THE APPRECIATION OF MUSIC

A *Living Method Course*

BOOKS BY ABRAM CHASINS

THE APPRECIATION OF MUSIC

A Living Method Course

by

ABRAM CHASINS

CROWN PUBLISHERS, INC.

NEW YORK

Acknowledgments

I first want to express appreciation to the officials of Vox Productions, Inc., and Everest Records for permission to use most of the excerpts on the accompanying records; to Siemens America Incorporated (Deutsche Grammophon Division) for their kind permission to use excerpts from their recordings of Haydn's *Eighty-eighth Symphony* and Stockhausen's *Kontakte;* and to Zara Nelsova for permission to use an excerpt from her masterly and otherwise unobtainable recording of Bloch's *Schelomo.**

Appreciation is also due to Nat Wartels and Herbert Michelman of Crown Publishers, Inc., for their warm understanding of my procrastination, and to my editor, Nick Lyons, who has earned my esteem and gratitude.

I also wish to thank Ann Sigmund for her helpful copy-editing, and Alan Mirken for assisting me in the use of the Vox and Everest catalogues.

Most especially, I am indebted to my late friend, the generous publisher Robert Simon, who invited me to attempt this album, which I now dedicate to his beloved memory.

Finally, let me emphasize that virtually everything I say stems from great teachers I was fortunate in having. Insofar as I succeed in making sense and speaking accurately, just so far can it be said that I am remembering them and endeavoring to repay them by sharing the enhanced joy that their guidance brought to my musical life.

* Unfortunately, copyright restrictions have made it impossible for us to obtain suitable recordings of such significant works as Debussy's *La Mer* and Ravel's *Daphnis and Chloe.*

Contents

Each record symbol ( ) in the text designates a musical illustration on the accompanying records; the first of these appears on page 4.

Approaching Music

In these days of tapeworm titles, this course might also be called "What the Music Lover Ought to Know That He Can Know Without Tying Himself Up in Knots of Technical Confusion." In simpler terms, this course is for those who enjoy listening to music and who would like to extend that enjoyment. I intend it as an approach to music for interested laymen rather than a text for advanced students or specialists. Its range, therefore, extends mainly to the symphonic repertory most frequently encountered by the concertgoer, radio listener, and record collector.

Short of extended formal schooling, there is but one "open sesame" to the musical experience: the development and quickening of the layman's ear, taste, and memory through familiarity with music itself. *The Appreciation of Music* seeks to aid the music lover to develop his standards of taste and of judgment; it seeks to encourage the range of his receptivity and to stimulate him to hear as a whole the symphonic works it discusses and illustrates; and finally, it hopes to prompt further adventures into the full world of music, only a small portion of which could be represented here.

A note about the compositions discussed and illustrated: The repertory requires me to concentrate on the towering works of musical literature, for the introduction of too many minor figures and works can muddy the mainstreams of art; details often involve the average listener beyond their esthetic worth and may perhaps diminish his interest. In my choices and commentaries, I have tried to be neither too esoteric for the untrained nor too elementary for the initiated. Should my readers find me saying familiar things, they should be regarded as gentle reminders of

things that we may know or ought to know, but that we sometimes forget.

Which compositions will the layman find most rewarding? This
he will have to discover for himself by listening to many works,
for acquaintance with a large canon of music is at the root of
musical taste. The history of music is the history of individual
works, and even among the masterpieces there exist degrees of
excellence. Fads and fetishes disappear and only that which is
"art" has remained. The timeless will be our chief concern here,
and the degree of the listener's sensitivity to masterpieces can be
measured by the extent to which they touch his heart, quicken
his pulse, and retain his interest.

How can this course intensify such reactions? Primarily, it can
introduce the pertinent facts of scales and keys, rhythm, melody,
harmony and counterpoint, tonality, and form, as they can be
heard in the music itself. Perhaps the most profitable way to
utilize this album is to read the text first. Then the commentary
should be re-read in conjunction with listening to music, for
inevitably all understanding of the language of music must begin
with hearing. In some special cases, to point out musical facts as
they occur, the commentary will actually accompany recorded
excerpts; at times, I shall illustrate passages on the piano; but
most often the music you hear will be examples from representative recordings. It is my hope that the unillustrated musical refer-
ences will only whet your desire to hear the works in their entirety.

Though I shall not assume that the reader knows how to read
notation or how to play an instrument, there is no doubt that his
listening ability will increase with some exercises in musical activity, such as singing in groups, learning a simple instrument, or
studying notation. But even this does not mean that he will become a better listener. Unfortunately, there is no guarantee of
that. It merely means that he will develop musical habits—and
things become easier when they become habitual.

On the other hand, anyone intent upon acquiring a professional grasp of music should find a good teacher, learn an instrument, practice regularly, and study theory and composition thoroughly. There is no other way. The mastery of a rich and complex art—which is as exacting and time-demanding a job as I know—requires guidance, practice, and experience. And for those who want to learn all the facts concerning music and musicians, there are first-rate musical histories and biographies available in a vast and vivid literature; philosophical and psychological studies of the artistic aims of the composers abound; and there are numerous precise technical analyses of the great musical compositions.

Though such books are indeed worthwhile, they belong to the world of words, and words have no power over the realm of instrumental sound; they can be useful only insofar as they lead us to think about music, and especially as they lead us to the music itself. Moreover, were it necessary to know all about the theory, facts, history, and technique of music in order to respond to it, then concertgoing, and phonograph and radio listening, would be restricted to a handful of trained musicians and musicologists. Modern musicology, notably in the writings of Ernest Newman and Donald Francis Tovey, has proved irrefutably the extraordinary accuracy throughout musical history of the plain man's instinctual judgment, unprejudiced by professionalism. Fortunately, fine music is enjoyable to all but the stone deaf.

This course, then, is for the music lover. It hopes to encourage his range of experience, to enlarge his realization that the inspirational quality he seeks from music does not exist in one style or one period alone, that the language of music is varied and evolving, and that each generation has added its contribution to the total. There is no greater pleasure than experiencing the beauty and proportionate rightness of first-rate music. Hopefully, *The Appreciation of Music* will further this experience.

THE LIVING LANGUAGE OF MUSIC

Music is both an art and a language. It is a "living" language in that it is constantly growing, and insofar as it speaks directly to the innate emotions of people of different centuries, nationalities, and sensibilities. Like all art, it is a form of communication between human beings. The material of human communication is the material of human meaning, and each medium of communication employs different materials. Sculpture, painting, and poetry employ stone, color, and words to communicate an artist's vision. The material of music is sound.

It is useful to think of music as a language in which each tone is a letter of the musical alphabet, groups of tones are the words, and recognizable melodies are the sentences. Small musical designs are short poems or stories, and large forms are the epic poems, the dramas, and the novels of music. The language even has its own grammar and syntax, its own style and principles.

No one knows why certain combinations of words are capable of firing our imaginations and moving us deeply, and why, when these same words are slightly, even scarcely, rearranged, they may mean nothing or something quite different. So it is in music. For example, let's select a few notes of the musical alphabet and observe their sound. 🔊 1

There we have a single line of melody, pleasant enough but not yet very meaningful or satisfying. Now let's organize it rhythmically. 🔊 2

Now let's hear it harmonized, expanded, and orchestrally colored. 🔊 3

I'm sure that you recognized the last movement of Mozart's *Fortieth Symphony in G Minor*. Now let's hear those identical opening notes, duplicated in another key, as organized by another composer. 🔊 4

That's the opening of Beethoven's first piano sonata, and he evidently loved the idea so much that he used it again in an orchestral work. 🔊 5

And what was that except the scherzo from the most famous of symphonies, Beethoven's *Fifth?* The extension of this theme is recalled by Beethoven in the finale, but in quite a different mood.

In order to appreciate this stroke of genius to the fullest, we have to hear the whole work, which of course applies to all the music excerpted on these discs. Here is another way in which music is a language, for the overall organization of a composition is similar to that of a novel or a drama in its succession of thoughts and events which succeed each other in logical sequences of cause and effect. Instead of words, the composer uses tonal images to express experience, emotions, and ideas in his own way. Not infrequently they turn out to be different interpretations of similar experiences, emotions, and ideas shared by others. Though there isn't very much new about love or death or war, something has remained to be told of each of these eternal themes by each great artist in turn, and whatever has been told with truth and passion and individuality has remained unique.

Music is its own language, and has the power of expressing less than words or more than words, but not specific meanings in the way words can. The language of music is learned exactly as a child learns any language—by hearing it—and by that process alone he comes not only to "understand" but also to express himself fluently long before he learns syntax or grammar. Thus, there are millions of people who can neither read music nor play music, but who love it very deeply. To say that such people are musically illiterate is as false as saying that a child who cannot read or write but who can carry on conversations hour after hour does not understand his language. He understands a great deal of it. But here is a significant difference between the language of music and the language of words: Every bit of knowledge and technique that we can acquire helps us to understand more precisely the explicit meaning of words we not only hear and read, but also construct and use ourselves. Music is a language that may suggest, but cannot possibly convey, explicit meaning unless we are directed by words to a specific meaning intended by the composer; and music is the language whose most significant aspects can be grasped without the ability either to speak it or to write it ourselves.

A sensitive appreciation of music stems from the ability to grasp its essentials: scales and keys, rhythm, melody, harmony and counterpoint, tonality, and structure, as well as such qualifying agents as tone color, texture, and orchestration. They constitute the materials of the language of music, and it is through this language that the masterpieces explain themselves fully to those who listen to music on its own terms. For though the language has been constantly enriched and enormously extended, and, in our time has become bewilderingly complex, still the elements remain the same. Thus, the listener has responded, even to those revolutionary works that renounced and swept away all those elements, according to his own capacity and experience. And in the art of music it is experience, call it familiarity if you will, that can expand our capacity to appreciate music that at one time we thought beyond us.

The Elements of Music

The elements of music must be heard before they can be fruit-fully described or discussed. Let us start immediately, then, by hearing a familiar melody from the opening movement of Schubert's *Unfinished Symphony.* 💿 6

The expression of that lovely tune is so natural to us, so appealing, that it is difficult to realize how relatively recent is the origin of the Western tonal system that made it possible to create and notate an *Unfinished Symphony,* how many centuries it took to work out its components. We twentieth-century music lovers speak of Vivaldi and Bach and Handel as old masters, but the eighteenth century was well under way before they were old enough to produce those mature works that provide the earliest examples of the compositions usually heard in our concert halls. This is not to imply that they were the first composers of mature masterpieces. Far from it. Preceding them were a host of supreme masters of ecclesiastic and secular vocal music, such as Palestrina, Monteverdi, and Byrd. Many others, including Gabrieli, Lully, Purcell, Sweelinck, and Alessandro Scarlatti, also left inexhaustible treasures of orchestral and operatic miniatures that were not only models for their own generations but also vital foreshadowings of the future. However, until recently, an acquaintance with the "Golden Age" was considered a scholarly specialty. Even today, the music of sixteenth- and seventeenth-century masters has not substantially entered the currently performed repertory.

More's the pity, for it embraces a wealth of music unsurpassed for purity, beauty, and variety. But our subject will be quite large and rich enough if we concentrate on the essentials of those

7

orchestral masterpieces that compose the bulk of symphonic programs.

SCALES AND KEYS

When we focus mainly on symphonic literature, it is reasonable to regard Bach as a beginning, because it was his *The Well-Tempered Clavier* that finally persuaded the musical world to adopt the tonal system on which all future Western music—except twentieth-century "atonal" compositions—was built. His first set of twenty-four *Preludes and Fugues,* in all the major and minor keys, emphatically showed how advantageous it was to relinquish an impractical system of tuning keyboard instruments that had restricted composers to the use of a limited number of keys.

The term "key" is an unusually accurate and helpful one in the generally loose language of music, for its meaning is akin to its usage in general conversation. The key of a composition actually opens the door for us to the harmonic home in which the composition lives, from which it departs, and to which it returns. The keys are alphabetically named, and their names are the starting note of their scales. There are two modes of key, major and minor. Since Bach, the scales of all keys have a uniform pattern and identical spacing that make it possible to play any composition in any other key merely by starting it on a different note.

However, the final choice of key entails some practical considerations. All of us have experienced the difficulty, or the impossibility, of singing melodies when some of the notes lie either too high or too low for our natural vocal range. If we start these same tunes on a lower or higher note, we may find them perfectly comfortable. For example, we have no trouble in singing "Silent Night" in the key of B-flat in this convenient registed.   ⬤ 7 Yet if we reproduce this identical tune by starting it either a fifth higher or a fourth lower in the key of F, we will find ourselves in trouble. Let's try it for fun. ⬤ 8

Instruments have similar problems. Some notes are simply not in their range. Further, the physical construction of certain instruments causes additional problems that make the performance of certain passages technically difficult, or even impossible, in certain keys—whereas in other keys they pose no problem whatsoever. These practical matters have sometimes compelled composers to alter the key in which they originally might have conceived their musical idea.

Nevertheless, these are minor problems when compared to the severe limitations suffered by Bach's contemporaries, to whom the possibility of ranging freely and excitingly throughout the whole range of keys was inconceivable until *The Well-Tempered Clavier* made it possible through an equal and systematized tuning. Bach's monumental work was not only a systematized demonstration of the advantages of equal tuning, but also a treasury of transcendental music. Were it not so, the musical world might never have troubled to adopt the practical purposes it demonstrated so eloquently. In addition, this collection could be said to have been "born for the keyboard," for it also exploited all the resources and potentialities of keyboard techniques. But Bach was not the actual inventor of the tuning system whose adoption altered the future of music. He was, rather, the powerful protagonist whose artistically beautiful work utilized an idea that had been available for at least a half-century—the idea of tuning keyboard instruments so that each octave would be divided into twelve equally spaced notes. ⬤ 9

Of course you recognize the sound we get on the piano by striking every white and black note. This is the chromatic scale that contains all the twelve notes used in Western music. The word "scale" comes from the Latin for "staircase," and it is appropriate because scales have a definite number of equally spaced steps placed one above the other. Each repetition of a scale's basic tones is like a flight of steps that we can either ascend or descend. The twelve chromatic tones we heard represent the new, well-tempered tuning system that at long last enabled composers—as Bach had demonstrated—to write in *all* the keys with equal freedom. These twelve tones and no others form the backbone of the music we know and love. Consequently, the appreciation of music begins with the recognition of this scale and the others that contain all the tonal material at the composers' disposal. Here are several examples that the chromatic scale stimulated.

"Habañera" from Bizet's *Carmen*. 10

"Evening Star" from Wagner's *Tannhäuser*. 11

And the witty "Flight of the Bumble Bee" from Rimsky-Korsakov's opera *Tsar Saltan,* almost entirely built on the chromatic interval. 12

Within the twelve tones of the chromatic scale are the seven tones of our familiar major and minor scales that for so many people carry only the unhappy associations of long hours of drudgery at an instrument. Nevertheless, nothing is more vital to the evolution of music, nothing more ever-present in the art of music, than the scales, which we could call the bloodstream flowing through the anatomy of music.

Here is the major scale. 13

And here are a few easily recognizable examples of its components as they rise and fall in important compositions.

The opening of the prelude to Wagner's *Die Meistersinger*. 14

There is an example from Beethoven of a descending major scale with a dramatic surprise at the end of it, an unexpected last note that does not belong to the scale, in the opening of "The Third Leonore Overture" from the opera *Fidelio*. 15

Endless examples exist to remind us that the scale is indeed the spinal column of all music, and of all kinds of music. Many will remember the popular old song "Raggin' the Scale." 16

Our final example is another popular song, though one more recent—Richard Rodgers' "Do-Re-Mi." ● 17

Now let's turn to the minor scale. Our Western system retained two from the many that we inherited from the Greeks. One, called the "harmonic minor," remains the same whether it is ascending or descending. ● 18

The harmonic minor is used in the opening solo of Mendelssohn's *G-Minor Piano Concerto.* ● 19

In the second movement of Tchaikovsky's *Violin Concerto,* it rises and falls. ● 20

It is in descending form in César Franck's *Symphonic Variations for Piano and Orchestra.* ● 21

Our other minor scale, called the "melodic minor," ascends in one way and descends in another. ● 22

Beethoven used the ascending form with dramatic effect in the *Third Piano Concerto,* as the solo enters. ● 23

Chopin used it enchantingly for the last movement of his *Second Piano Concerto,* and then rounded out the phrase with an expressive descending chromatic scale. ● 24

And now for a final and revealing illustration—treatments by various composers of four identical notes of the descending major scale. ● 25

From the sixteenth century, John Dowland's famous song, "Awake My Love." ● 26

From the eighteenth century, "Lift Up Your Heads" from Handel's *Messiah.* ● 27

A nineteenth-century example, and a strange one, the famous left-hand octave passage from Chopin's *Polonaise in A-Flat.* ● 28

And finally, another nineteenth-century example, and the richest one, wherein Tchaikovsky makes this basic pattern do triple duty as the principal theme of the second, third, and fourth movements of his *Fourth Symphony,* each transformed with inexhaustible resourcefulness. Later in the last movement,

Tchaikovsky discloses the source of his inspiration, a Russian folk tune whose first four notes are the notes of our pattern but in the descending form of the melodic minor scale.   29

Let's pause a moment now, and ask ourselves what we can observe from these samplings of the ways in which the successive tones of scales, or portions of them, were organized by composers into melodies or melodic fragments. How strikingly different those identical patterns emerged! Yet all were constructed from the same tonal material. Obviously, many qualifying elements worked to set their effect and emotional content worlds apart.

The conclusion should be obvious. Melody, so fundamental and familiar to us, is considerably more than a single and singable strand of sound; it is far less detached than it appears when we attempt to dissect music into isolated elements. Such dissection has value for specialists, who must examine music through microscopes, but to the average music lover it can be misleading, even if it were scientific—which it is not. Even the most naïve listener, whose musical experience is limited to popular ballads, cannot possibly hear a melody as inseparable from rhythm and harmony. Let me illustrate this.   30

You recognize that tune, don't you? You don't? Well let me play the tune as Stephen Foster wrote it.   31

Of course! It's "Oh! Susanna." Even though I first played the exact notes of its melody, you could not recognize it because its other elements were distorted. Let me play it once more.   32

I am sure that the end of this last illustration was a rude shock to you, wasn't it? We do not have to be professors of harmony to know that something was radically wrong. We would have to be tone deaf, or even stone deaf, not to hear that there was no relationship at all, direct or indirect, between that last chord I played and what went before it. What makes us know this is an innate harmonic sensibility, a sense of tonality, to which the untrained listener is as susceptible as the most astute musician.

Tonality performs somewhat the same sort of function in music that the horizon line performs in painting. When we say that a piece of music in classic tonality is in a certain key, we may reasonably expect it to begin in that key, travel through other keys for the sake of contrast, and eventually return to the home key. In short, tonality is to our ears what perspective is to our eyes. It is comparable to the fixed point of a canvas, to which the painter relates everything that belongs to his picture.

Although there is no more complicated as well as fascinating aspect of music than tonality, though it is almost impossible to describe verbally, the listener experiences little difficulty in appreciating its overall effect. This is particularly so in spacious works, which take us on exciting adventures through a wide range of different keys before staging the most dramatic effect of tonality —the welcome return to the home key.

Tonality is therefore primarily the art of key relations, and the composer has no more powerful means of expression and interest and surprise at his command. It is also the aspect of music that perhaps places the greatest demands on the listener's attention. But this should not frighten us, for every great composer establishes his home key so solidly, so unmistakably, that the listener needs no theoretical knowledge to recognize and to respond to changes of key. These key changes called "modulations" are grasped almost instinctually whether they are in juxtaposition or even at considerable distance from the home key or from each other, or whether they are closely related or widely contrasting.

Since we can hear the full effect of this process of changing key, or modulation, only in longer passages, I shall delay illustrating it until we get to those large-scale works in which its magical effect can be most fully savored. As we explore the many ways in which composers develop their ideas into more and more spacious forms, we will see that the element of tonality is as inseparable from musical design as rhythm, melody, and harmony.

Among the earliest and most significant masters who insisted on the firm establishment of tonality was the Italian composer

Antonio Vivaldi, born about a decade before Bach. In the whole history of music, few creative contributions were more inventive, prolific, and far-reaching, or more neglected, than the life's work of this Venetian genius. Fortunately, through our century's tremendous interest in the Baroque styles, Vivaldi's music is now enjoying a renewed life and extensive representation in concert and radio programs, and on recordings. Only recently has the world come to realize the extraordinary caliber and extent of Vivaldi's art, and the incalculable influence it exercised on his Italian, French, English, and German contemporaries, and most particularly on the music of Bach.

One characteristic illustration, the opening of Vivaldi's *Eleventh Violin Concerto,* is enough to show us Vivaldi's strength of tonal feeling, his power of solidly planting a whole key in the listener's ear. 🎻 33

This typical Vivaldi theme asserts the tonality of the movement so strongly because its material is entirely generated from the fundamental chord and scale of his key, which in this case is E minor. This is the fundamental chord of E minor. 🎻 34

Vivaldi merely broke it up by making one note follow another. 🎻 35

He then continued to assert the key by using the ascending form of its melodic scale. 🎻 36

Bach loved this idea enough to imitate it identically, except in the major tonality, in his *Violin Concerto in E Major.* 🎻 37

But Vivaldi and Bach were hardly the only composers who saw the beauty and the value of themes that were made up of the basic chords and scales of a chosen tonality. We encounter such themes constantly throughout eighteenth- and nineteenth-century music. Mozart's *D-Major Violin Concerto* (K. 218) provides another striking example of its use. 🎻 38

To continue chronologically, let me remind you of Illustration 23—the piano-solo opening of Beethoven's *Third Concerto,* consisting solely of the dramatic use of the C-minor scale and a broken chord. Near the opening of Schubert's *Fifth Symphony,* we find an especially graceful treatment of the broken chord of his tonality, B-flat major; and Brahms often uses this kind of material, as in the openings of his *Second Piano Concerto,* and his last three symphonies. Music is full of themes of this type, and its greatest masterpieces are invariably marked by firmness of tonality, whose most vigorous innovator was Vivaldi.

The other essential features of Vivaldi's art and influence stem from the fact that he was among the great violin virtuosos of his time. The very core of his orchestra was the string section. His marvelous knowledge of what it was possible to extract from a four-part string ensemble, and his unflagging imagination regarding the unprobed potentialities of string playing and technique, all led to incalculably far-reaching results. He initiated a whole new instrumental style, and was, in fact, the most important precursor of the symphony. But all his innovations, all his technical skills, would have been of little interest to his contemporaries and followers, would be totally unknown to us, were it not that in his greatest works Vivaldi was a supreme creator, a lyrical and vital poet.

All the elements of music—no matter how efficiently related and organized—hold little or no significance for us, and no power whatsoever to stir us, without the mysterious spark that Duke Ellington described concisely and colorfully in his dance lyric, "It Don't Mean a Thing If it Ain't Got That Swing." In other words—less idiomatic but more usually applied to the music we are talking about—no composition, no matter how intellectually impressive it might be, is anything more than an exercise or an experiment if it lacks inspiration. This is the life-giving force that makes each work an individual expression of timeless human emotions, which dictates the composer's methods of dealing with all the elements of music as they interact upon one another in those works we call masterpieces.

RHYTHM

Once we recognize great music as the inspired integration of inseparable elements, then it becomes safe and useful to study the nature of each element and its contribution to the whole. First in importance among these equals is rhythm. No element in any art is so basic as rhythm, and nothing is so emotionally appealing and physically exciting to our entire being. No natural phenomenon is more apparent in the universe or in life; we find it in the systematic rotation of the stars and the seasons, in the ebb and flow of tides, and in the heart beats and breath of all living things. The word "rhythm" itself comes from the Greek for "measured motion."

Hardly anyone is without a built-in mechanism we call a "sense of rhythm," and it is easy to understand why we are no less susceptible to its hypnotic power than the savage who came to his idols dancing to the beat of drums. Rhythm reaches directly into the nerves and brain cells that control the rhythmic patterns of our own muscular and emotional make-ups.

The rhythmic patterns to which we respond most instinctively are the strong, regular accents of dance rhythms that range from the most obvious and unchanging thump of a bass drum in a march to the most subtle effects of structure and contrast in a symphony. In music, therefore, rhythm is the dimension that takes up every aspect of time, and since music by its very nature is a process existing *in time,* rhythm is an inexhaustible subject, indivisible from every other musical element.

When people tell us that what they really like about music is rhythm, they are usually referring to the simple and strongly accented beat that we find in a Sousa march. ◗ 39

Or they may be referring to the waltz rhythm that we find in a Strauss waltz. ◗ 40

All of us react instinctively to the double rhythm of a march, and to the triple rhythm of a waltz. Our pulse, heart beat, and breathing respond to these rhythms autonomically as our moods respond to their character and pace. No wonder they became the basic metrical units on which all other musical rhythms are based. They are physically and psychologically appealing, they make music easy to follow, and their regularity enables large groups of singers and instrumentalists to keep together easily.

However, human beings eventually tire of anything that is undeviating. We need stability, but we also crave flexibility and surprise. It was inevitable, then, that the routine inflexibility of "*one,* two, *one* two" or "*one,* two three, *one,* two, three" finally produced monotony, despite the remarkable resources that composers displayed in obtaining variety within the tyrannic metrical confines of twos and threes and their multiples.

As the musical art developed, rhythm, like all other musical elements, expanded in the direction of contrast and complication. Curiously, it was not until the twentieth century that Western music disclosed a rhythmic ingenuity and intricacy comparable to that displayed by primitive African and Asiatic drummers, obviously dating from unrecorded time and having passed from one generation to the next by rote. Actually, the escape from a humdrum "beat" that brought vitality to art-music through irregular accentuation was no radical revolution, for each aspect of it had a long origin in the folk music of every land. For example, the deliberate displacement of normally accented strong beats to the usually weak beats, or "off" beats as we call them, had its roots in West Africa. We Americans know it best as syncopation, and as the main feature of jazz. "One, *two,* three *four,* five, *six,* seven *eight.*" An excellent example of it is to be found in George Gershwin's "Rhapsody in Blue." ◗ 41

The colorful device of shifting accents away from the strong and expected beats was used by the oldest masters with great effect. There is a subtle example in Bach's *Italian Concerto.* ◗ 42

We meet a famous case of that <u>oompah</u> rhythm, called a "riff" in American jazz, at the end of the second movement of Beethoven's *Fifth Symphony*. 🎵 43

The *Sixth Hungarian Rhapsody* of Liszt introduces an interesting syncopation. 🎵 44

There is an unusual example from a famous Chopin waltz, where we hear the first phrase in normal waltz rhythm with the usual first beat accented, and the next little phrase—the answering phrase you would call it—in mazurka rhythm, the Polish dance step that makes the dancer land with the accent on the third beat. 🎵 45

We have been talking about musical rhythm in terms of only two of its elements so far—time and accents. Rhythm also embraces many other elements: tempo, which indicates the pace or the approximate pace at which a piece is to be played; the hurrying ahead or slowing down of a tempo once it has been established; phrasing, which is comparable to punctuation in literature and to breathing points or stopping points when we read something aloud; and still other elements, whose technical names and complex definitions tell us less about the music than the music itself.

About a century ago, the regularity of fundamental dance rhythms, in units of twos and threes and their multiples, began to be broken up by composers of art-music. In the second movement of Tchaikovsky's *Pathétique Symphony,* the composer, instead of using the rhythm, "*one,* two, *one,* two" or "*one,* two, three," combined the rhythms in a most original fashion, "one, two, one, two, three, one, two, one, two, three"—making five, of course, "one, two, three, four, five, one, two, three, four, five." Listen to it. 🎵 46

This novel rhythm is so easy to follow that music lovers are often astonished when its irregularity is pointed out to them. That is because of Tchaikovsky's ingenuity in holding everything together through an overall design consisting of square eight-bar phrases—call them sentences or units—which maintain a uniform pattern throughout. Nothing in the whole evolution of musical art is more pertinent to our era than the way earlier artists took careful account of the way people use their ears, and thus successfully extended the horizons of every musical element. Many of these attempts were no less stimulated by the needs and desires of the artists to produce something new, than by their public's eager appetite for newness. These efforts to find ever more rhythmic variety has resulted in some astounding music in our century. Here is an example from Bartók. 47 We can recognize in this next example from George Gershwin's *Piano Concerto,* in which he demonstrated how eight could be divided into three plus five, the "*one,* two, three, *one,* two, three, four, five" of the Charleston rhythm. 48

An entirely different sort of metrical freedom—very fluid, the rhythm only subtly suggested—can be heard in "Iberia" from Debussy's *Images.* 49

The rhythmic effect of all these last examples—the Tchaikovsky, Bartók, Gershwin, and Debussy illustrations—certainly take us far from the obvious accents of a Sousa march or a Strauss waltz. Yet even the most naïve listener's ear can follow them quite easily, not only because we are relieved from the monotony of a crude beat that would grow unbearable if it went on for too long, not only because we are charmed by the endless variety that comes from the flexibility of rhythm itself, but also because all the other elements involved—melody, harmony, shape, orchestration, color —can readily be grasped as logical artistic extensions of the language of music as it has been spoken for the past three centuries.

The complete destruction of rhythmic regularity came together with the frontal attack upon tradition that shook the twentieth-century world in every phase of art, science, sociology, politics, and life itself. The change took on the pace and violence of revolution. The crucial event that altered the course of musical history was the sensational Paris premiere in 1913 of *The Rite of Spring* by Stravinsky. The most radical and startling characteristic of this shattering masterpiece was a new concept of rhythm, as we can hear in "The Sacrificial Dance." Hardly one measure of that barbaric and jagged music corresponds rhythmically to the measure before or after, and yet, somehow it manages to attain an extraordinary balance, an asymmetrical balance.   50

As we hear these rhythmic illustrations, from the bold rhythm of the Sousa march to the astonishingly complex range of rhythmic variety in the Stravinsky dance, it becomes clear that in each case there is much more going on than just rhythm. While the effect of that rhythm is primitive and hypnotic, the rhythm alone could not hold our interest for very long. For music as we know it and respond to it can never consist entirely of pure rhythm any more than it can consist of pure melody without some rhythmic organization that gives it shape and makes it recognizable; or without the harmony, actual or implied, that is supplied by our mind's ear when we hear the melody. The total effect of music is the interplay of all these elements as they interact upon one another. Let me illustrate this process with the opening section of the second movement of Schumann's *Piano Concerto*.   51

Now what can this tell us? Plenty. For example, as we concentrate on the important elements of this music, one at a time, how astonishing it is to discover that the rhythm in Schumann's time signature is identical with Sousa's march from *El Capitan*. Why do they sound so different? Because the time signature represents only the rhythmic organization of the composer's ideas; it does not show whether a piece is fast or slow any more than it shows that it is loud or soft, or aggressive or lyrical, or to be played steadily or flexibly.

These significant details are determined by the style and character of the composition, by the composer's intentions and directions, and by the interpreter's methods and skills in expressing them accurately and eloquently. And this leads us to the realization that musical rhythm is not like the ticking of a clock or a metronome unless it purposely maintains the steady pace that we use when we march or dance. Otherwise, rhythmic freedom is as fundamental to music as it is to life, to the very pace of our walking or speaking or breathing, depending on whether we are calm or excited, whether we mean to be humorous or serious. So it is in music that the naked, rhythmic division reflects no inflexible fact. It is a common-sense matter of conveniently conveying the time element of a rhythmic plan, subject to the emotional content of a composition.

MELODY

One of the chief characteristics of every form of art is the organization of its materials into meaningful patterns that our ears and eyes can grasp and remember. Rhythm, slow or fast, regular or irregular, simple or complex, is the organization of the time pattern of music, and therefore governs the time relationships of melody. Melody is an element of its own. Characterized by the rise and fall of the human voice, it is the organization of successive single tones. There was a time in music when it was just that, pure unaccompanied vocal melody. 🔊 52

However, the development during the past few centuries of the harmonic system that has dominated musical literature normally prevents our ears from hearing a melody as detached from its surroundings. The music that appeals most to most of us is music in which we can find accompanied melodies that we call beautiful. Although there is no disputing tastes, most of us understand each other perfectly when we think of a melody or a tune or a theme as an appealing musical idea that has fixed itself firmly in our minds and hearts, that keeps running through our heads, that we can swing or whistle or pick out on an instrument. Melody, therefore, is the recognizable surface of all the other basic elements of music. Most often it appears as the top layer of a musical composition, as in the third movement of Mendelssohn's *Italian Symphony*. 🔊 53

Sometimes we find it in an inner part, as in the third movement of Brahms's *Third Symphony* sung by the cello section.   54

And sometimes we find it in the bass, as in the second movement of Schumann's *Rhenish Symphony*.   55

These three melodic examples are the products of three highly individual masters of nineteenth-century Romanticism, whose language and methods can be said to have evolved logically from artistic styles and values that radiated from the classic masters of the previous century.

At the end of an entire century of Romanticism stand three other gigantic symphonic figures, Tchaikovsky, Strauss, and Debussy, each with widely different philosophies, styles, methods, and temperaments. From a melodic point of view, nowhere do we find more powerful, more eloquent themes than in the music of Peter Tchaikovsky, and nowhere has his genius shown itself more compellingly than in the *Pathétique Symphony,* perhaps the most original, lyrical, and dramatic of the Russian master's symphonic works. One of its finest features is the luscious theme in the first movement.   56

This had been called "a tune to end all such tunes," and that is almost literally true because no subsequent composer has yet succeeded in creating another theme of that sort which does not sound "Petered"-down.

Speaking of tunes that sound diluted, how should we regard the common practice of expropriating instrumental themes from the masters, setting them to words, and using this material in popular songs? Let's examine a few of them and see how they bear out the definition of melody as a recognizable succession of notes whose entire effect can be completely transformed by alterations of rhythm, pace, harmony, or shape.

Our example from Schubert's *Unfinished Symphony* serves as a case in point. "My Song of Love" was the popular version of that heavenly tune by Schubert.   57

Surely you noticed how plodding those graceful rhythms of

Schubert become in the song. And how little variety there is in the harmony. The resulting devitalizations stem from the commercial necessity to avoid complication, and from the prefabricated conventional form into which most popular composers pour materials, which leave no more room for rhythmic or harmonic surprises than for any other kind of deviation from the familiar. In popular music, clichés are safer and more salable than subtleties. But is it not obvious to the music lover how drastically such alterations diminish the innate beauty of imaginative music? Precisely the loveliest features of Schubert's melody, its charming little twists and unexpected turns, are carefully suppressed.

We find the same dilution in the popular version of Chopin's *Fantaisie-Impromptu,* whose central section became "I'm Always Chasing Rainbows." Here is the original version. ◆ 58

And this is the version of the popular song. ◆ 59

I'm sure you will agree that the popular version of the Chopin tune fares no better than did the Schubert. But there is a more primary difference between these popular songs and their classical models. In classical music, themes are but the raw material of large structures. Some of them are very arresting, while others are not impressive in themselves; and still others have the brilliance of epigrams. Even the most scintillating series of epigrams will not make a well-constructed piece of music, any more than they will make a well-constructed short story, let alone a novel or a drama. In a popular version of a great theme, we meet merely a theme, and whether or not it has been left intact, that is usually the beginning and the end of it. In a work of art, we meet not only a thematic idea, or several ideas, but also the spacious unfolding of their potentialities through enriching development. When we come to the subject of form, we will take a special delight in the methods through which composers prolong ideas or fragments of ideas and expand them into large, convincing, and dramatic designs.

Having just heard examples of familiar themes by two masters that were compressed and weakened in popular versions, let us now hear some familiar themes that were expanded and ennobled by imaginative and gifted composers. Here is an excellent example of that process, using the Israeli National Anthem.　● 60

Here is how Smetana developed this idea in his tone poem "Die Moldau."　● 61

The richest and freest developments of single tunes into large and independent structures are found in the great sets of variations by the masters. We will get to them presently.

Early in our century, Richard Strauss crowned a vital chapter in the development of melodic imagery in a series of astonishing works that brought the art of orchestration to a new brilliance, color, and pulsation. These works also demonstrate a magnificent sense of movement that Strauss maintains throughout his large forms, and the forms themselves are strikingly original. Finally, there is Strauss's fantastic invention of a glittering array of themes that are seldom complete, but rather are fragments of themes, often powerfully suggestive of common and easily identifiable sounds which somehow remain remarkably independent of their illustrative stimulus.

Let's hear how Strauss's thematic and orchestral resources disclose themselves immediately in the opening of *Don Juan,* the very first of his tone poems that contributed so substantially to musical evolution.　● 62

These bold, entrancing ideas and still others continue on their magical course to a final shattering and memorable climax. The luxuriant harmonic and melodic invention of the early Strauss, the riotous orchestral colors, the sensational power of composition, showed themselves ever more flamboyantly in the succeeding tone poems that flashed like meteors across the musical horizon and established him as a leader of modern music. Nevertheless, despite the daring and distinction of Strauss's imagination and technique, his art primarily extended former and easily traceable lines of evolution. The inspiration for his symphonic poems derived from Berlioz; his sense of continuity and movement could only be called Wagnerian; the Quixotic melodies were rooted in Romanticism; and beneath the fast-shifting and brilliantly colored harmonies was the foundation of German Classicism. Eventually, this major creator of our century, who began as a rebel, who triumphed both as a supreme orchestral and operatic figure, lived to see himself denigrated as a conventional rather than original artist.

Claude Debussy was unique in his melodic invention, and starkly original in effecting its interaction with the other elements of music. It was at the Symbolist poet Mallarmé's home that the young French musician met the fascinating figures of Impressionist poetry and painting who gathered nightly to discuss their philosophy, aims, and methods. Although their talents were highly individual and their techniques greatly diversified, they were all united in a common desire to attain a style that would suggest and symbolize rather than concretely describe, that would capture the fleeting but intense moments of experience, the fugitive impressions and sensations of life bathed in exquisite, exotic, and elusive colors.

In this atmosphere, Debussy found himself and his life's mission. Embracing the philosophy and spirit of this new French art, captivated by its masterpieces, Debussy went on to create their musical equivalents and to become not only the prophet of musical Impressionism but also the prophet of all that we loosely call "modern music." With the startling opening of *The Afternoon of a Faun,* the thirty-year-old Debussy served notice on the world that it was witnessing a turning point in musical history. 🎨 63

Now, in what ways was this music so epoch-making? First, the solo-flute melody is so vague, so fugitive and fragmentary. It hasn't the clear-cut design of the melodies we have heard until now, nor is it developed into fragments of itself the way they are. And when we first hear it, our minds are unable to anticipate or to supply harmonies beneath it, because the organization of its tones do not conform to the behavior of the classical scales that are the basis of our harmonic sense. When Debussy's distinctive harmonies appear, the chords themselves are not entirely unfamiliar, for behind their novel harmonic sensations lurk similar meanings and directions that we have experienced in classical and romantic schemes, though now the chords move up or down with a completely new independence. As for rhythmic character, this music certainly has anything but a regular and steady momentum. It wanders, it flickers, it advances and recedes with enormous freedom. Furthermore, its overall orchestral coloring is as different from the music which preceded it as the canvas of a Cézanne is different from the canvas of a Rembrandt. We no longer hear the gigantic chords, the huge sonorities of the mammoth orchestra of Richard Strauss. Instead, all is subtlety and delicacy and economy. The instrumental sonorities, from the quietest to the mightiest, shimmer with a thousand coloristic effects. Finally, its wayward designs are unlike the compact compositional grouping of ideas that we find in the symphony, the cause-and-effect relationship of clear-cut musical units that evolve into larger ones and eventually form constructions whose full impact appears as the conclusion of a logical sequence of dramatic events.

Debussy's music, on the other hand, is concerned with its texture from moment to moment; yet it is anything but formless. It has a structural coherence that is as convincing as its stylistic integrity. Perhaps the most fascinating thing about Debussy's art is its perfect expression and undeviating reflection of his milieu. And perhaps the most instructive aspect of his art, because it has so much to teach us about the contemporary scene, is that though Debussy was one of the few truly innovating and original geniuses who cut away from the main lines, we can recognize in his music a paradoxical kinship to both Wagner and Tchaikovsky, and a wide range of other influences, including the resources of ancient music. For example, he used the oriental five-note scale which we find on the black notes of our piano. You know that sound, of course. You may have played games with it on the piano. Even Chopin did, in his brilliant "Black-Key Etude." 64

And so did the great Impressionist, Ravel, in his amusing sketch "The Empress of the Pagodas," from his *Mother Goose Suite.* 65

There was a time when Debussy reduced his melodic and harmonic schemes to an alternation between this scale and one called the "whole-tone scale," for the obvious reason that it contains no half-tones or any wider skip than a whole tone. 66

There are many subtle examples of Debussy's transparent use of all scales integrated happily within one work, as in *Images.* 67

Debussy was one of those revolutionists without the "r." Despite his visionary genius, his fierce independence was at all times guided and matched by a wide knowledge of an equally wide variety of sources and resources of the immediate and distant past.

The consummate skill of both Strauss and Debussy finally reveals the expansion rather than the destruction of firmly established traditions. In their idiomatic masterpieces, both advanced the melodic cause no less than those of the other musical elements.

HARMONY AND COUNTERPOINT

When we sound a note by vibrating a string, it is a scientific fact that not only does the string produce the fundamental tone that we hear, but also a rising succession of overtones. This phenomenon is the basis of that intricate system of tonal relationships which comprises "harmony." It is also the basis of the contention that certain aspects of harmony are rooted or latent in certain aspects of nature. Such facts and theories may serve to explain at least some of the reasons why harmony is among the most powerfully expressive elements of Western music.

A workable definition of harmony is "the simultaneous combination of two or more sounds of different pitch, in contrast to melody, which consists of single tones." This is an incomplete definition, though, because the term harmony can be applied to any musical combination that sounds well. Technically, however, harmony can be obtained by means of what appear to be two contrasting methods. First, through solid blocks of chords that have little or no independence from the tunes they are enriching. We find an illustration of this purely harmonic aspect of music in the second movement of Beethoven's *Third Piano Concerto.* 68

This simultaneous sound of dependent chords usually heard below a melody and played solidly together constitutes the "vertical aspect" of harmony. The other method of obtaining harmony is by means of a combination of melodies. This is the "horizontal aspect" of harmony called "counterpoint"—in other words, point counter point, or note against note. 69

The orchestral prelude that Wagner wrote for his opera *Die Meistersinger* clearly illustrates the nature and significance of harmony and counterpoint in their fullest maturity after the slow and painful evolution of many centuries. Primarily, Wagner uses three themes that should be familiar to you. Let me illustrate them. 70

At the end of this prelude, Wagner combines these three tunes wonderfully, in the classical manner of creating counterpoint. But this is not pure classical counterpoint, for in addition to the horizontal progression and momentum of these melodies that he combines to make chords, he also adds notes to the chords in order to smoothen the harmonic progression, and to amplify the sound as luxuriantly as possible. Before we go further, let's hear this particular section. 71

That is a magnificent sound, isn't it? But what elements contribute to its magnificence? The recognizable melodies are indeed beautiful, but isn't it also the fascinating patterns and colors of everything else that enhance the melodies? And surely you noticed that the harmonies do not merely accompany one dominant melody, but are actually melodies of their own, with their own independent lives.

In short, as we found in the behavior and characteristics of rhythm and melody, musical elements are always interacting upon one another. Actually, no worse blunder was committed by musical historians than to detach harmony from counterpoint, and we will only compound the error if we separate them from form, texture, tonality, and from the other major elements of music.

Admittedly the subject is complex. Yet I am certain that even those who never before heard Beethoven's *Third Concerto* had no trouble in detaching the melody from the solid blocks of Beethoven's harmony. And I am equally certain that even the complicated web of sound in Wagner's "Prelude" to *Die Meistersinger* was easily grasped through its inherent logic and beauty.

Insofar as the facts of harmony are concerned, "learning the names of the chords" is not, in my opinion, likely to serve the music lover's chief objectives. A famous theorist once asked Mendelssohn whether he knew the name of the unusual first chord of his celebrated "Wedding March." ⬤ 72

Mendelssohn replied that he neither knew nor cared. Evidently, this did not hinder the composer's capacity to create that music, any more than it hampered the capacity of generations of music lovers to enjoy it. In fact, the chord that provoked the question seems like the simplest and most natural thing in the world to even the least musical man of our day, so thorough has been the nature of harmonic evolution.

Nevertheless, the simple blocks of harmonies that constitute the underpinning of our ballads and folk songs somehow never lose their appeal for even the most sophisticated of us, and their very simplicity makes them extremely useful as illustrations that may increase our musical sensibility. Here, for instance, is the opening of "Way Down Upon the Swanee River" by Stephen Foster. ⬤ 73

Now let me remind you of another famous tune—Dvořák's "Humoresque." ⬤ 74

Below those melodies I played the simultaneous sounds that comprise the "vertical aspect" of harmony. Now let's leave out the harmonies and keep just the two tunes we heard, putting them together in order to see what happens. ⬤ 75

In an admittedly naïve way, they go well together, don't they? In fact, we can call them "harmonious." That sort of simple combination is not only a favorite trick, but an ancient one—the simultaneous sounding of two or more melodies independent of each other, creating counterpoint. Another ancient device, possibly the earliest of all art forms, is starting a melody, and then, at a harmoniously convenient distance, reproducing it exactly to accompany itself. Everyone has done this with "Frère Jacques." ⬤ 76

Most frequently, counterpoint is defined as "the art of combining melodies." But this definition proves inadequate when we recognize that the horizontal weaving of melodic strands inevitably results in vertical harmony whenever they meet, as we discovered with that combination of "Way Down Upon the Swanee River" and "Humoresque." Now, if three or four or five people came upon a stage and sang anything that came into their heads, in complete indifference to what the other ones were singing, it wouldn't be likely to make much sense, would it? Actually, then, counterpoint is the art of combining melodies that together will produce unity and coherence—which is another way of saying that the total impression of good counterpoint should be good harmony.

Any psychologist will tell you that it is an impossible feat for the human mind to follow separately each melodic strand of a many-voiced piece of counterpoint. Though we can hear any number of things simultaneously, we cannot concentrate on the complex progression of more than two. The layman therefore has the advantage over the analytical professional who tries to follow the individual and complex contrapuntal lines of a multi-voiced composition, for the layman will enjoy the most important quality, the total sonorities resulting from good melodies imaginatively and skillfully combined. Musical literature contains no greater example of the vertical and horizontal aspects of harmony in stunningly contrasted sequence than in Bach's *B-Minor Mass.* The chordal introduction for chorus and orchestra immediately leads to an orchestral fugue-theme that begins the "Kyrie" with majestic vigor.   77

Bach's crystal-clear polyphony gives us an excellent opportunity to notice that fugue textures are those in which all the parts are of more or less equal importance; this enables us to appreciate fully why the period dominated by contrapuntal music, and brought to so triumphant a maturity by Bach and Handel, was appropriately called "the golden age of counterpoint." But we must be careful not to conclude that all the art-music of that period was contrapuntal, any more than we should conclude that all the music of the nineteenth century was harmonic. One cannot safely generalize about any aspect of art, let alone from having heard only one or two examples of any given texture, form, or period from a composer's work. Rather, our curiosity should be stimulated to extend our experience to many works of similar categories, each of which will constantly manifest both resemblances that charm us because they are familiar, and differences that provide new interest to our listening. The assertion, for instance, that composers of the Baroque and pre-Baroque periods conceived music horizontally or contrapuntally, rather than vertically or harmonically, is simply not tenable; it is readily refuted by a short phrase by the sixteenth-century composer Palestrina.   78

If that sounds familiar, it is because you remember a significant phrase from the last movement of Brahms's *First Symphony*. 79

The Palestrina and the Brahms are identical, are they not? It would be illogical of us to be at the mercy of the dates of their composition, and therefore to explain Palestrina's music as contrapuntally organized, and the identical music by Brahms as harmonically organized. If we allow the sounds to speak for themselves, we will describe each passage as a series of harmonies that move along by means of the momentum and the progression of the four melodies within their chords.

In short, harmony and counterpoint are inseparables: There is little profit and less illumination in asking which came first. Further, the sounds that these elements make become intelligible and rememberable and satisfying through two other elements—tonality and form. Eventually, I shall have more to say about the peculiar vitality that is breathed into harmony by counterpoint, an issue that should culminate in a discussion of fugue, the musical composition whose harmonies are built entirely through contrapuntal organization; but it will be most helpful to discuss fugue under the heading of "Musical Form."

Every art, and each aspect of an art, has its own rules. The rules of harmony importantly include consonance and dissonance. Though consonance is commonly defined as "sounds that are agreeable," and dissonance as "sounds that are disagreeable," the terms are actually relative, and mean very little when lifted out of context. Listen, for example, to this series of agreeable sounds called consonances. 80

Such a series of consonances are agreeable enough, of course, but if I kept them up for any length of time, I am sure you would find them not only boring but even disagreeable—far more boring and disagreeable, in fact, than the whole series of so-called "dissonances" with which Stravinsky opens *Petrouchka*. 81

Clearly, this is very pungent stuff, and anything but disagreeable. Yet if we continued to hear the unbroken series of dissonances, they too would become extremely tiresome.

The last two illustrations should convincingly refute in sound those two definitions quoted. Actually, consonance and dissonance are a psychological matter with which we deal every day —an extension of the pleasure and pain principle. Sunshine is appreciated more when it is alternated with rain, and heat is particularly enjoyed after cold; the best way to enjoy a fine meal is first to feel twinges of hunger. When we experience discord in music, just as when we experience discord in our human relations, we make every effort to resolve it so as to regain the harmony of which we have been deprived. This is exactly how consonance and dissonance operate. All the music we adore is full of consonance and dissonance, and it is the skillful blending and balancing of the driving, forward momentum of dissonances and the tranquil or victorious resolution of consonances that help to bring us the cumulative satisfactions from great music whose foundations are solidly laid.

No element of music has changed so rapidly and so frequently as harmony. So rapid, in fact, have its changes been, that the dissonances of one day virtually became the consonances of the next. Later, it will be profitable to examine the knotty subject of dissonant harmony as it exists in a large group of twentieth-century composers who repudiated not only harmony as we know it, but the whole musical language and technique they inherited.

Challenging tradition is hardly a new process; nor is experimentation, which, to some degree, is part and parcel of every creator's search for truth. In harmony, the break with tradition was evidenced by a speeding up of the distance between dissonances until the classical distinction between consonance and dissonance was actually abandoned by a large number of contemporary composers in a large number of compositions. The fact that virtually none of these works has been taken to the heart of the great public indicates that what has not disappeared is the need for some tonal center, some home base, to which the listener can relate, no matter what wild experiences he may be exposed to by an imaginative composer.

This, too, is very much akin to what happens in our daily lives. Today we can get to faraway places in a short time, and often we feel like strangers until we get used to our surroundings. Being far from home, perhaps for a long time, can provide thrilling adventures; but few of us are willing to abandon our homes. Most of us enjoy getting back again all the more.

TONALITY

Tonality, as my previous brief reference to it indicated, is that important musical element which establishes a recognizable tonal center—the home base in which a composition dwells, from which it departs for its adventures, and to which it finally returns. It is as difficult to define in words as it is easy to enjoy spontaneously. Except for a highly experimental segment of twentieth-century composition, the whole literature of music could not have been conceived or implemented except within the system of consonance and dissonance; and this system could not have existed at all without the harmonic guidance of tonality.

Before attempting to describe or define tonality in more detail, let me demonstrate that you possess an innate sense of tonality, exactly in the way that the character in a Molière comedy discovered that he had been talking prose all his life without knowing it. Here is the beginning of Brahms's best-known waltz.   82

With this opening, Brahms establishes in our minds and memories, the home key, the tonal center of his composition—and a bit of variety to keep our interest. But just as it could grow boring if we stayed home all the time, so it would be boring to remain constantly in the same key.

To create new interest, Brahms takes us on an adventure through modulation—a change of key, a change of tonal environment. A modulation may take us quite far afield and for a long time, or it may keep us fairly close to home, and serve as an interesting incident, so to speak, in the course of a short journey. This is purely a matter of proportions, and nothing distinguishes the greatest masters more than the exactitude of their architectural sense and their understanding of the range over which a listener depends upon his memory. Brahms's knowledge was second to none in these matters, and in this little waltz he planned our itinerary perfectly. He takes us just far enough and long enough away from home, and then takes us back, not alone to the home harmony, but also to the original melody, this time gracefully embellished, though easily recognizable. Our musical example illustrates this experience.   83

I am certain that instinctively you felt the home ground, the wandering away from it, and the welcome return home. Perhaps another description, through the best and nearest analogy I know, will help clarify the phenomenon of tonality further. Tonality, as I previously suggested, is to music what perspective is to painting—that horizon point, a vanishing point, from which our senses measure all other details of the whole canvas, and which therefore is inseparable from them. However, there is one radical difference between pictorial perspective and musical tonality. Perspective is an existing scientific fact whether or not an artist chooses to use it; whereas tonality, as we know it, is a man-made art that by its satisfying coherence has dominated music for almost as many centuries as perspective has dominated Western painting.

The Brahms waltz just illustrated is a short piece, and in an art that moves in time, this brevity limits the opportunity for harmonic adventuring, for that long-distance wandering which a large-scale work not only allows but demands. No musical resource has more architectural power than significant key relationships and modulations to effect the delay and therefore to intensify the expectation of the most dramatic and exciting of all experiences to be had from large-form symphonic works: the return home. As the long-range aspect of harmony, tonality is obviously inseparable from structure and form. This constitutes not only another corroboration of the interaction of every element of music, but also an important reminder that we cannot grasp any work of art unless we take it as a whole.

Before leaving the subject of tonality, we might clear up the popular misconception that a major key is a happy key and a minor key a sad key. Take, for instance, the tune "Annie Laurie."

84

This tune is in the major tonality, but one would hardly say that it is a gay tune. Here is one in minor—"Charlie Is My Darling."   85

That is hardly a sad tune. Now, let's test some classical examples. Here is the opening of the second movement of Haydn's famous *Eighty-eighth Symphony,* in the major tonality.   86

There are not many examples in all of music that one could describe as more wistful, more full of pathos. When Brahms heard it, he said, "I want my *Ninth Symphony* to be just like that." Finally, here is a classical piece in the minor key, Mendelssohn's scherzo from *A Midsummer Night's Dream.*   87

Is this not truly joyful music? What makes it so joyous? Certainly not because it happens to be in minor, but because the mood is gay and the tempo swift, because the tone color and the texture of the orchestration are so delicious, so feathery, so translucent.

So far we have found that melody and rhythm are as inseparable as harmony from counterpoint, and that the sounds they make become meaningful through the element of tonality. But perhaps nothing is more obvious in music than the fact that as one tone moves to another tone, there is not only motion but design, from the simple shape of a melodic fragment to the complicated organization of a gigantic structure of a large-scale composition. This observation leads directly to the broad and vital subject of musical form, a subject so large as to span the entire realm of music, and to require a separate section.

Form

Perhaps the most central element of music, surely the most misunderstood, is the element of form. In an art that must be followed phrase by phrase and that progresses in time, it is of cardinal importance.

Nothing is more fundamental or useful to human experience than the way we learn to recognize the shapes and sounds of things, for this enables us to identify and remember them. And when we say that something we have seen or heard is shapeless and formless, we do not mean that it has *no* plan, but that as a whole its plan has remained unclear, that it has failed to convince us, to satisfy us, or to establish a recognizable design.

In art, there is no such thing as a disembodied plan or form. The form of an art work arises from the organization of all its materials, and so once again we are confronted with an essential element of music, inseparable from the other parts of a composition.

The word "composing" derives from the Latin, meaning "to put together." Though no one needs to be persuaded of the crucial role played by construction in all the arts, we must make a clear distinction between those arts that move in time, such as drama or music, whose designs make claims on our memory because they gradually unfold before us moment by moment, and those such as painting or sculpture, which can be experienced all at once.

In music, form is essentially the art of movement. We enjoy it only in constant connection with melody, harmony, rhythm, and other elements and details; they, in turn, not only provide pleasure in themselves but also in their relation to the entire structure. Perhaps the greatest damage to our understanding of the architectural variety and freedoms within similarly named masterpieces that differ widely from each other has been caused by the view of musical forms as uniformly set patterns, or as prefabricated molds into which composers pour creative liquids. Such a view contradicts the primary principles of art—namely, that each work of art is an individual case, that no two are identical, and that the form of a work of art is developed organically from the inherent nature of its materials.

Music reveals its design, its shape, its structure, from point to point in each work. All the musical knowledge in the world would not enable us to anticipate or to account for every note and every phrase in a composition. Too often, in fact, the generalizations compiled from other works are applied, misleadingly, to materials that exist in an endless variety of relationships; and thus our attention is focused on peripheral similarities rather than on crucial differences. And finally, we can miss the forest for the trees, precisely as we would miss the total impression of a huge mural if we examined it through a microscope, or would fail to grasp the emotional content of a drama if we parsed it sentence by sentence.

One of the constant struggles of composers, from earliest times, has been to extend the whole range of their materials, and to attain an ever-larger time scale for compositions while yet holding the memory and attention of listeners. In the sixteenth century, the listener's memory was not tapped or taxed beyond the links that extended merely from one accent to the next. It took over a century to train ears to retain harmonic or rhythmic relations over a melodic span of eight measures, which corresponds to the first section of every popular tune of our time. And it took another century before the art of Haydn, Mozart, and Beethoven originated and demonstrated the dramatic dimensions that called with confidence upon the listener's ability to remember and relate effects whose seeds had been planted a quarter of an hour earlier.

The vast architectonics of the great Viennese school did not stem directly from the Baroque school, whose methods made far fewer demands upon the listener's memory. Although at this point musical architecture took a totally new direction, Bach and Handel had already asserted themselves so powerfully in every other practical way that the gigantic achievements of the Teutonic intellect for the next two centuries cannot properly remain dissociated from them.

Before the new influences came upon the scene, Bach and Handel had already summarized and breathed fresh life into whatever they found to utilize and revitalize through their unique imaginations and powers of organization. In the process, they brought order to the chaos that resulted when instrumental music began to emancipate itself from the domination of vocal music and its dependence upon verbal texts. For them, instruments became voices with supernatural ranges and colors, for which they developed sizable art forms consisting of groups of individual movements conceived as a whole.

Let's see what we can discover by illustrating sections from Bach's *Orchestral Suite in D Major,* one of the earliest masterpieces to demonstrate the sharp contrasts within sublime unity achievable in nonvocal, absolute music. This piece begins with an overture, a seventeenth-century French art form that was a sort of detachable instrumental introduction to an opera or a dramatic composition. Bach transformed the overture as he transformed every art form he ever used, and in the same way— by intensifying its essential character and defining it more sharply than anyone before him. In the "French Overture" you will see more vividly than in any of its predecessors the majestic scene as the nobility march rhythmically to take seats before the curtain rises. ●● 88

Then follows a lively movement which indicates that the curtain has risen on the *corps de ballet,* which will entertain the listeners before they settle down to hear something more serious. You should especially notice the contrasting textures of these movements when you hear the entire composition.

You will note that the rollicking first movement is in fugal style. Such a discussion of a contrapuntal theme by a definite number of voices has been called, wrongly, "fugue form." A fugue is not a definite "form" like a fourteen-line sonnet, but a texture, like blank verse or prose. A piece of music written in fugue texture can therefore be a two-voiced piano composition that lasts two minutes, a massive, many-voiced structure for full chorus and orchestra, or a normal-sized last movement, as in Bach's *Concerto for Two Pianos and Orchestra,* whose witty subject was Illustration 69. Here is the conclusion of the joyous finale, which builds steadily to a grand climax.   89

What we can tell immediately is the character and length of the melodic idea, appropriately called "the subject," and also the number of characters who are going to discuss it; for a composition that is written *in fugue* always has a definite number of voices that are held to be self-sufficient so that any further material is outside the scheme.

This digression was necessary to demonstrate that there are two aspects to musical form—its texture and its shape. To return to Bach's *Third Suite,* the next movement, the Air, is among the purest examples of his melodic style; and the last three movements, here very briefly excerpted, consist of a gavotte, a bourrée, and a gigue—three rhythmically contrasting dances.   90

This variegated scheme was the natural outcome of the composer's search for ever more proportion and contrast. Actually, we can understand the problem perfectly if we ask ourselves what else was a composer to do who had fully exploited a particular idea within the space of one short movement, and wanted to produce a work on a larger scale. He wrote another movement; then another; and still others. Most of them were in a spirited or solemn dance rhythm, but composers began to interpolate still other movements in other meters and moods to attain greater length and variety. Some of these movements were free fantasies that served as connecting links; others were serious dances, like the loure or the pavane; and sometimes this string of separate

and contrasted movements ended with a chaconne or a passacaglia, stately dances in triple time, with marked processional
character. ⬤ 91

The early age of instrumental virtuosity also gave rise to other
popular forms. The theme and variations was among the most
ancient in origin, for what is more natural than to take an idea
and then to elaborate on it? Among the most effective and familiar examples is the theme and variations scheme of the first
movement of Mozart's widely-played *Sonata in A* (K. 331).
⬤ 92

Perhaps the favorite instrumental form of the first part of the
eighteenth century was the "concerto grosso," to which Vivaldi
first brought such a wealth and variety of vital expression. It is
easy to understand the instantaneousness of the appeal of the
concerto grosso, for nothing in human history is more exciting
or basic than the antithesis of the individual versus the crowd,
of small human forces against large forces. In music, it began
to be expressed very early in the vocal arias of Alessandro Scarlatti and in a variety of instrumental concerto forms that reached
a dramatic peak in the solo concertos of Mozart, Beethoven,
and Brahms. Nevertheless, even their ancestor, the concerto
grosso, where the opposition consists of a small group of orchestral soloists pitted against the main body of the orchestra,
depended entirely upon the concerto principle, the age-old contention that progresses from unequivocal opposition, through
compromise, to final and harmonious appeasement. The whole
idea is perfectly illustrated in the first movement of Bach's
Second Brandenburg Concerto for four solo instruments—trum-
pet, violin, flute, and oboe—and orchestra. ⬤ 93

These forms, and still others, were incorporated and ennobled
by Bach and Handel in supreme examples of a primarily poly-
phonic art that was consummated by them and that also culminated with them. What else was transpiring during their life-
times was a complete transformation of the whole art of music;
polyphony was becoming as academic as its theological texts had

become outmoded. This could not have remained totally unknown to them. Certainly not to Bach, whose sons Carl Philipp
Emanuel and Johann Christian were contributing notably to this
transformation. Nevertheless, the new developments remained a
matter of indifference to both Baroque masters. Bach, with astonishing humility, merely said that musical art was advancing
to a very great height—indeed, beyond his ability to incorporate
it. This fact makes a straight-line view of musical history quite
false, for Bach's and Handel's magnificent achievements were not
direct preparations for the radical change that took place in the
language of music.

That change stemmed from the Neapolitan vocal art founded
a full generation earlier by Alessandro Scarlatti, quite independent of Bach and Handel, which bypassed them both and passed
into the art of Haydn and Mozart. In fact, the whole art of
music was on the threshold of a stupendous change through a
dramatic new development, the sonata style. The moment it
arose in the latter part of the eighteenth century, with Haydn
and Mozart, instrumental music took on more intensity and
architectural power than any earlier music.

This does not mean that the significant works of Bach and
Handel were lacking in thrilling emotional and structural quali-
ties, but even their mightiest designs were necessarily bounded
by the resources at their command before the essential features
of sonata principles were discovered. The impact of their massive
designs was their cumulative effect, mainly developed and extended from one central idea within one texture. But even in
those movements in which they used more than one idea, they
did not have the means to attain the vital elements of dramatic
action sustained through entire movements on a huge time scale
which the sonata style made possible.

SONATA FORMS

The short schemes and simple layouts of a Chopin prelude or
a Schubert song are easy to follow and to remember, and they

can be beautiful, dazzling, or even forceful. But the significant expression of profound thoughts and emotions takes ample time. Since time is the constant and determining element of musical design, the development of the sonata forms—those architectural schemes that enabled instrumental music to assume dimensions adequate to the most dramatic demands—was the milestone of musical history most directly related to concert music.

The word "sonata" originally meant a piece played by instruments, as distinguished from a "cantata," a piece sung. Its schemes have ranged from the brief and brilliant single movements for harpsicord by Domenico Scarlatti to the passionate and spacious four-movement *"Kreutzer" Sonata* for violin and piano by Beethoven. For us, the term "sonata" will indicate a work of at least two, and more usually four, well-contrasted movements, and we will take the word "movement" to mean a member of a sonata that forms a self-sufficient musical design.

The sonata has also been called an instrumental work for not more than two instruments. This is too narrow a view, for structurally, from Haydn onwards a "trio" is actually a sonata for three instruments, a "quartet" a sonata for four instruments, a "symphony" a sonata for orchestra, and a "concerto" a sonata for one or more solo instruments with orchestra. It is also useful to keep in mind that the difference between works designed for a few instruments, such as trios and quartets, and those designed for many instruments, such as concertos and symphonies, is not that of dimension. The difference lies primarily in the volume of tone obtainable and in the range of tone color available.

The primary principle that we find exemplified in all those successful works we call masterpieces is that of variety within unity. In symphonic music we find it in its highest state of organization in supreme sonatas whose forms have arisen from the inherent nature of their raw material.

We know that the raw material of music is sound, that its smallest unit is one note, and that its smallest shape is a group of notes called a figure. Very well. But the ease with which this has led to the misconception that large structures are "built up" from small scraps of themes has hindered generations of music lovers from a full appreciation of many great works that are chiefly remarkable for the length and breadth of their concept.

Few laymen and too few musicians have escaped this most damaging of all clichés through the most frequently cited example—the opening phrase of Beethoven's *Fifth Symphony*. Not only is the monumental first movement of this expansive symphony claimed to be erected from the initial figure of its four famous taps, but all recurrences of these notes or their rhythm in the later movements have been made to account for the unity of the whole composition. The heresy is worth refuting to show the crucial difference between a creation and a concoction. Let's recall Beethoven's four-note figure from the *Fifth Symphony*. ● 94

Clearly, no great symphonic movement could be built up from such a figure any more than the George Washington Bridge could be conceived and constructed from bolt to bolt. What should concern us, if we are truly to appreciate musical rhetoric, are no less comprehensive issues than complete and organized ideas.

When we listen to the opening passage of a musical work, we must allow it time to explain itself. It is only essential to know that melodies that consist of more than one phrase invariably fall into sections that are either complete or incomplete This is best illustrated through the simplest and most familiar melodies. Let's use "London Bridge Is Falling Down" first. ● 95

This musical idea, like a short sentence broken by a comma, is complete enough to make sense. Whether a composer chooses to leave well enough alone, or to repeat an idea, or to go on to another idea, is his business—provided that he has not left us hanging in midair. In "London Bridge," that's all there is—there isn't any more. In Stephen Foster's "Oh! Susanna," we find a more extended plan. Here is the first idea. ● 96

That's rather like a question, isn't it? It leaves us hanging in midair for an answer. Why? Because our instinctive sense of tonality makes us feel unsatisfied. The idea is incomplete and obviously must continue, so Foster decides to repeat the basic material, though he alters the last few notes to resolve his question. ⬤ 97

He could stop here, but he wants us to become more familiar with this opening statement; so he repeats it, with two tiny rhythmic changes. ⬤ 98

Though Foster's entire theme bore repetition, left us with a feeling of satisfaction, and could have stopped right here, the composer wanted to expand his piece and build a larger structure. Could he have repeated any of his former material? Try it and you will see that he could not, not yet anyway, without ruining his piece through excessive repetition. Instead, he presents a new idea, a contrasting idea, somewhat more lyrical, that also takes us on a harmonic adventure by wandering a bit away from the home key. ⬤ 99

Finally, he rounds everything out by returning to his original theme in its original key. ⬤ 100

Foster first established an idea and a home base. By repeating his first idea, he gave us a feeling of balance. Through contrast he satisfied our need for variety. With the return of the original idea and tonality, and through symmetry of mood, form, and material, he fulfilled our desire for unity.

Precisely the basic ingredients that produce this feeling of rightness and inevitability and completeness in the plainest tune do so also in the mightiest symphony. The simple scheme we just heard is the microcosm, we could say, of the most elaborate musical designs that constantly display the important principles of symmetry and of variety within unity.

THE FIRST MOVEMENT

The first movement of a sonata, whether it is called a symphony or a concerto, is the most highly organized of all musical forms.

It owes its structural power to the three main divisions that we found in "Oh! Susanna"—exposition, development, and recapitulation. The exposition obviously exposes the main material and gives us a strong feeling of the home key. The development promotes the possibilities of the materials that were exposed in the first part and also takes us on a harmonic adventure into other keys. The recapitulation also acts according to its dictionary meaning: It restates and summarizes the exposition, and, in music, provides the special satisfaction of returning us to the home key. When the composer feels that this has not given us a sufficient effect of finality, he will add a little tail called a "coda" to complete the design.

If this description has given the deceptive impression that every first movement in the sonata style is identical, you will be all the more delighted to discover in one composition after another how ingeniously all great composers vary, in every imaginable way, and in many more ways that are quite unimaginable, in their utilization of this basic scheme.

The very first thing that a musical work can offer is an introduction. It may have an impressive architectural character, as in the introduction to Mozart's *E-Flat Symphony* (K. 543). Or it may be quite short and merely preludial, as in the introduction to Haydn's *Military Symphony*. 101

It may even be as monumental and tragic as the introduction to Brahms's *First Symphony*. 102

Obviously, some introductions are purely introductory, merely setting the stage, while others have more dramatic significance and dimension. However, once we acquire the excellent habit of listening to music as a process in time, we will never feel the necessity of knowing in advance what it is we are listening to from the outset. Music always reveals what it is at the proper time, and nothing explains more quickly or more clearly that it is not an independent movement in itself, but a preface to something larger, than a musical introduction. Here is another example, the introduction to Tchaikovsky's *Pathétique Symphony*. 103

I also illustrated the actual beginning of the symphony, to point up what to me has always been a fascinating feature of this opening. Stylistically, Tchaikovsky is as remote from Haydn as one could imagine. Yet, there is little doubt that the character of Tchaikovsky's introduction and of the relation of its materials to the main body of the movement show startling similarity to Haydn's symphonic methods, as in his *Ninety-eighth Symphony*. It would be of value and interest for you to compare the shadowy mood and color of both introductions. Note that they both foreshadow the main themes, which turn out to be the same themes in vigorous new versions.

Of course there are many works without any introduction whatsoever, like Mozart's *G-Minor Symphony*. You will recall the opening; there is no mistaking it for an introduction. 104

Apart from its beauty, it owns a fantastic sense of momentum, precisely that mastery of movement which Beethoven developed with such drama and power, nowhere more poignantly than in his *Fourth Symphony*. The introduction to this composition is truly an *introduction* as is immediately apparent by its color and character. 105

Now note how Beethoven propels us with a new tempo, new mood, and new spirit into the main body of what we instantly recognize as the real start of the first movement. 106

Then, in the exposition, we come to another theme—a pastoral, contrasting theme. 107

No rules govern the number of themes to be heard in the exposition of a sonata, or in any other part of a composition. And so, in many compositions you will hear little fragments of melodic ideas, perhaps little transitions between one melody and another which do not deserve to be called themes at all. The listener should do his best to remember what he can, to be alert to new happenings, and to sensitize himself to changes of key, because a fresh tonality—as I pointed out before—is the start of dramatic action in the sonata form.

The sonata exposition contains two main groups, either of which can contain any number of themes. The first group establishes the home key, and the second a different key. To test this, go back to the last two musical illustrations—and observe the additional contrasts that Beethoven achieves through his use of different instrumental combinations. The strings announced the spinning theme of the first group; and the second group opened as a conversation between the bassoon, oboe, and flute—perfect colors for the simpler, quieter character of this contrasting section. And as you listen to the entire symphony, several new themes will appear before the end of the exposition, and when you get to know them, it will delight you to see what happens to them.

After the exposition comes the development, built on a much larger scale than the exposition so as to provide enough time to develop its melodic material, to break up its themes into terse figures, to rebuild them into new shapes, to recombine them so as to give them new rhythm and new meaning, but, above all, to enable all these ideas to range widely over many different keys in order to increase our sense of distance away from the home key. Sometimes a composer will introduce a new theme, to prolong the adventure and to delay to the last possible moment the return home. Whatever the means, the objective is to heighten the excitement of that moment of recapitulation. The alert listener will relish hearing the first movement of Beethoven's *Fourth Symphony,* in which the development lingers before the portals of the recapitulation in a key so opposed to the opening tonality that the return home provides a special effect.

This return home illustrates one of the many dramatic possibilities of the recapitulation of the first-movement sonata form. Another well worth anticipating and enjoying is the process by which the lyrical contrasting group is most often restated in the home key instead of in the key of its original appearance.

The very end of the movement illustrates what a composer might do when he feels that a movement will not end satisfactorily on its own momentum. He can add a little tail, a coda— which is what Beethoven did in this movement. ⬤ 108

We have had to limit ourselves to the illustration of certain notable features of the first movement of a great work. But remember: this is not a stereotyped mold into which any other first movement will fit. For instance, the gigantic introduction to the *Ninth Symphony,* which plunges us so deeply and immediately into a drama, scarcely seems like an introduction at first. Our attitude should always be, what's next? What surprise is in store for us through the composer's imagination? When you hear Beethoven's *Fourth Symphony* in its entirety, notice that the recapitulation of the first movement happens to be a fairly exact repetition of the exposition. But you will hear many symphonies and concertos whose recapitulations differ widely from the original statement, just as the returns will vary from tremendous lengths of anticipation to shocking abruptness, as in Beethoven's *Ninth Symphony.* In the "normal" first movement of a sonata scheme, we will constantly find just such latitude within its typical features. But "normal," here, should be taken as it is used in a favorite story of mine. Bernard Shaw once said that he had learned the true definition of the word from his ophthalmologist, who after an eye examination commented, "You know, Mr. Shaw, you have normal twenty-twenty vision in both eyes, and it is most unusual."

THE SECOND MOVEMENT

The second movement, usually the "slow movement" of a sonata, symphony, or concerto, will invariably show slight differences, that make all the difference. It may consist merely of the statement and brief development of one simple tune, as in Haydn's *Military Symphony.* ⬤ 109

It may consist of several complex themes, greatly expanded and with extraordinary freedom, as in the slow movement of Brahms's *Second Symphony*. It may be a set of variations on one theme, as in Beethoven's *Appassionata Sonata,* or on two alternating themes, as in his *Seventh Symphony*. Or it may turn out to be a spacious and leisurely scheme with a wealth of luxuriant themes developed along the lines of a first-movement scheme, as in Beethoven's *Second Symphony*. In short, we will meet an opulent variety of designs which constantly defy the rules.

Customarily, though, a slow movement is predominantly poetic and meditative, so as to provide a sufficiently lyrical contrast to the essentially dramatic quality of the first movement. Sometimes, it plunges us into a very distant key that contributes still further contrast, as in the slow movement of Brahms's *First Symphony*. Sometimes, the composer leads us more gradually to a remote key by modulation. This is best described by the sounds themselves. Here is a lovely example from Dvořák's *New World Symphony,* the end of the first movement and the start of the second. ◖110

Dvořák has led us gently to this unexpected and mysterious harmony, and only now is he ready to disclose the beautiful and famous theme of his slow movement, sung on the English horn. ◖111

Sometimes, a lyrical slow movement will grow intensely dramatic, as we discover in the momentary blaze of triumph in Beethoven's *Fifth Symphony*. But in such cases, it is usually brief, because in a successful sonata scheme each movement must make its unique contribution, and it is not the function of the second movement to compete dramatically with the first.

The slow movement of Brahms's *First Symphony* is a useful lesson to anyone who imagines that mastery of form is achievable through expert craftsmanship alone. Craftsmanship is also a result of inspiration, as Beethoven demonstrated with a technique that virtually changed with the dramatic demands of each new work. Brahms was no less ruthless toward conventions that he found inadequate to the fulfillment of his materials. The freedom of his art forms is vividly illustrated in the slow movement of his *First Symphony*, full of incalculable invention. It may be useful to comment briefly while the sounds themselves are in progress. ⬤112

This is how the first movement ends. The second movement begins with a quiet theme sung by the bassoons and violins. Notice not only this lovely opening idea, but also its tonality, so coolly remote from that of the first movement. Brahms now springs a surprise. He doesn't continue calmly but introduces an impassioned little digression. Quiet is restored again. A new little idea follows, united to a brief phrase from the opening theme. Now the strings continue with a series of flowing passages that rise and fall and flow on in the most unexpected manner. And so the movement continues on with numerous, unforeseen beauties.

When you hear this movement in its entirety you will notice how its material reappears in all sorts of wonderful ways, as florid solos by the woodwinds and the strings with gorgeous new accompaniments, now contracted, now expanded. Throughout, Brahms constantly provides some fresh delight, some new poetic harmony or combination of colors, ranging from delicate and shadowy tints, to flaming splashes of passionate power.

Again, we will also find it rewarding to listen to the sheer instrumental sound of this music, for each orchestral style has its own characteristic texture and color. The physical evolution of the orchestra from the sixteenth century, when a tiny group of instruments accompanied a vocalist, to the gigantic forces of the twentieth century, has been the constant enlargement of its personnel, the volume and variety of sounds possible to produce, and the ever-increasing technical improvement of instruments and the virtuosity of their players. Since music exists primarily in performance, each of these developments was inherent to the very conception of composition, and in the nineteenth century contributed to the dramatization of music.

THE MINUET AND THE SCHERZO

For at least a half-century, the last half of the eighteenth, the structural unity of a full-sized dramatic sonata scheme had always included a minuet. There are good reasons why this dance movement, which remained undeveloped and undecorated—why it alone among all the dance movements of a suite survived to become incorporated in the sonata. Its form is the neatest, the most symmetrical of all, and very simple: a tune, a contrasting tune, and an exact repeat of the first—like the arrangement of a vase between two candlesticks. The minuet's graceful mood and tempo also made it just the right thing in the right place—aristocratic and animated enough to contrast with a slow movement, but not so spirited as to spoil or threaten the effect of a brilliant finale.

Before hearing a delicious specimen, it will be helpful to recall the characteristic feature of the concerto grosso, marked by a small group of solo instruments alternating with the full body of the orchestra. This method of obtaining contrast was utilized in the minuet by assigning its middle section to three instruments only, which explains why this center portion came to be called a "trio." Let's hear an example of the old-type minuet, from Haydn's *Military Symphony,* consisting of a lively first theme, an ingratiating and beautifully contrasted trio, and an exact repeat of the first part. ◄► 113

I selected that particular minuet because it provides so extreme a comparison with what happened later to the minuet in the hands of Beethoven, who expanded it into the scherzo. In the process, he even changed the character of the scherzo, which in Italian means "joke" or "jest." In his mature works, Beethoven transformed his scherzos into symphonic movements of tremendous dimension and force.

Though we cannot demonstrate them now, you should listen to the tiny scherzo from Beethoven's *Second Symphony,* and then the scherzo from his *Ninth.* The first is not nearly so large as some of Haydn's mature minuets, but it is typical of the young Beethoven. Then compare that scherzo by the thirty-two-year-old composer with that of his *Ninth Symphony,* conceived by the profound visionary at fifty-four. Though they have a remarkably similar melodic pattern, note the world of difference. Astonishing features also arise in the scherzos of Beethoven's intervening works, as he was driven to ever new discoveries by the emotional demands of his ideas. In his *Fourth Symphony,* for example, he expanded the scherzo scheme by stating the whole movement, trio and all, twice over, ending off in a breathlessly quiet and abridged third statement of the main theme, plus a few extra and enchanting measures of farewell.

In the scherzo of the *Fifth Symphony,* partially illustrated earlier, Beethoven abandons this third return, and for a marvelous reason. First, he plunges us into darkness with a mysterious new section full of terror, and then in a thrilling crescendo leads us into the blazing and sunlit finale; then, right in the middle of this triumphant movement comes the surprise, the stroke of genius in the delayed reappearance of the scherzo theme, but this time the terror is gone. Donald Francis Tovey commented on this miraculous moment with rare perception when he said, "Beethoven shows us that his is the one and only solution which confirms the truth of the former terror and the security of the present triumph, but no lesser artist could have found it."

Few artists after Beethoven could escape his influence. Yet, paradoxically, it freed and inspired Dvořák to produce a scherzo of magnificent power and originality in his *New World Symphony.* As we hear the scherzo theme, it should recall our "Frère Jacques" trick in the way that the theme for flute and oboe keeps imitating itself. ⬤ 114

Now we meet a contrasting theme in the major key. ⬤ 115

Is *that* the trio? Well, we might think so, until we allow the music to unfold and make clear that it was merely an interlude leading into the real trio, a delightful theme for wind instruments that we will realize is the real thing because of its obvious importance. It has traveled a long distance from its ancestor for three instruments, it lives in a remote key, and it is ushered in by a reminiscence of the opening theme of the first movement of this symphony. ●● 116

As for the rest of this glorious symphony, it is equally unpredictable, for it is utterly unique. Dvořák was a true genius, many of whose less famous works are at least equally masterful and will handsomely reward anyone's investigation. So will a wealth of music also to be found under the title of "scherzo," which exists in remarkable variety, from the lyric brilliance and beauty of Mendelssohn's scherzos, through the somewhat ghostlike and ominous scherzos of Chopin, to the most elaborate architectures that expressed the highest degree of dramatic power in the sonata-form scherzos of Beethoven, Brahms, and Dvořák.

THE LAST MOVEMENT

We have seen that some balanced plan underlies every well-constructed musical form, no matter how small or large; that in full-size sonata schemes we will hear either a three-movement composition with a spacious and dramatic first movement and a lyrical slow movement, or a four- or five-movement composition that contains a minuet or scherzo to provide dance rhythms to contrast with the surrounding movements. For the last movement of sonata schemes, various designs have served composers to round out significant instrumental works so as to leave us finally convinced of the logic and unity of their tonal dramas.

We shall find, as we come to the *dénouement* of those dramas known as symphonies and concertos, that even the largest of the sonata forms exemplifies the principle behind its smallest part— unity within variety. The word *"dénouement"*—so important in the language of the theatre—is appropriate here, because the last movement of the sonata form presents the composer with the identical problems that face a dramatist in summarizing the action of his play. The dramatist must unite everything that went before. He must find a clear and satisfactory solution to a complex situation. He must dissolve the tensions that have accumulated, and resolve the conflicts that have arisen. Finally, he must hold our attention to the very end and leave us convinced of the coherence and unity of his whole work. So must the composer.

But at this point the analogy breaks down. In the theatre, a joyous ending to a tragedy would strike us as absurd and completely false, but in music all but a handful of the sonata forms end triumphantly. Every symphony of Beethoven, surely the most tragic of composers, ends in a blaze of affirmation, and the most profoundly tragic of all, the *Ninth,* concludes with an "Ode to Joy."

The "happy ending" also belongs to every Beethoven concerto, but that is less surprising, for it is impossible to find any concerto by any composer that does not have a light-hearted finale. Why do all concertos end brilliantly? Because of the need to affirm the conciliation of conflicting forces. But in addition, not even those of us who resist the heresy that the purpose of concertos is technical display can fail to realize that this form is the most sensational expression of all sonata schemes and that anything short of a spectacular conclusion would be a frustrating anti-climax.

What sort of materials, what sort of designs, have composers used to sum up such works—to pull the whole plot together, so to speak—excitingly and entertainingly? We will find some of the answers if we return to the theatre analogy again. Clearly, a dramatist would be making a great mistake if, in the last act, he introduced dramatic situations which had been fully exploited in previous acts or if he initiated a complicated situation that would take considerable time to develop and would put a further strain on our attention and memory. The *dénouement* is a time for clarification, not involvement. Such principles apply to drama and music alike. All successful last acts, like all successful last movements, adhere to these principles of simplification.

This suggests why so many composers concluded so many works in what is called the "rondo style." In music, the name and the characteristics of the rondo form derive from the ancient French poetic form that consists of a brief but complete phrase that came 'round and 'round again, alternating with several contrasting couplets. But the mature rondo pattern within the sonata scheme lends itself to no easy description.

In fact, rondo forms are not even confined to last movements. In Beethoven's *Fourth Symphony*, for example, the slow second movement is cast in an extremely spacious rondo form with connecting links between its eloquent main theme and its two episodes. The attentive listener will be further intrigued and captivated to discover that when the main theme first returns it is beautifully embellished, and that finally, after a totally unexpected and full recapitulation of the opening material, there follows a mysterious coda that merely alludes briefly to the main idea.

In addition, the rondo is not less subject to a great composer's use of surprise then anything else in music. Beethoven was greatly influenced by both Haydn's and Mozart's treatments of rondo finales in the richest vein of comedy, though never twice alike. But Beethoven transformed the rondo as he did the minuet, by enlargement, expansion, and by occasional alteration of its originally playful character. When we observe his utilization of the broad rondo scheme in both the soul-stirring lyricism of the *Eroica Symphony*'s slow movement and in the yodelling gaiety of his *Pastoral Symphony*'s finale, it should alert us always to expect the unexpected and to take freedom of form entirely for granted.

Though orthodoxy continues to insist that the rondo finale discloses "no significant changes of key or thematic developments," two familiar examples will suffice to show otherwise, and to clarify the point musically. The first, the finale of Haydn's

One Hundred and First Symphony, reveals how the inexhaustibly imaginative "Father of the Symphony" could introduce a typically compact rondo theme and then take off on all sorts of unpredictable adventures, as capricious as they are easy to follow. Observe the following features the next time you hear it.

Obviously, we first hear the rondo theme. Then what? A first episode? Oh, no, it turns out to be a spacious transition passage to another key. Now what? Haydn seems to be making a new theme out of the materials of his first. Ah, there's the new theme, and if you listen carefully, you will hear that it is connected to the second part of the rondo theme. At last, in pure rondo style, the main theme returns; but see how Haydn ornaments the last part of it. Then there is a truly new stormy episode in the minor key. At this point, we expect to return to the main theme. It's there, all right, but it's on the bottom, and on the top is still another theme, and Haydn treats them in royal fugal style. Finally we get the satisfaction of hearing the main theme again, bringing everything to a brilliant end.

Now let us illustrate some pointed features of the great rondo that concludes Beethoven's *Third Piano Concerto,* which markedly influenced later composers, notably Brahms in the rondo finale of his *First Piano Concerto.* 117

The spirited main theme enters. The first surprise—Beethoven expands it. Now he writes a little flourish, a little cadenza before completing the opening idea.

Now, a transition to the first energetic episode.

Here is an unexpected little episode that leads back to the expected return.

Now, we meet a spacious episode that provides a charming contrast in character, color, and key.

Following this, does Beethoven return to the main theme in the main key? Hardly. We hear only the beginning of it in a fresh tonality which is used as the subject for a little fugue. The piano then intervenes assertively and carries us to a distant key, which is particularly effective when we hear the whole concerto because it is in the tonality of the slow movement.

This movement illustrates impressively the way in which Beethoven constantly sought new ways to heighten the effect of his repetitions. How exciting his harmonic adventures make both the anticipation of the return and the actual return of his rondo theme in the home key. This is followed by a sonata-like recapitulation that contributes to the dimension of this movement. Later, after an ornamental cadenza, Beethoven adds an extended coda in which the piano starts off with a marvelous pun on the main theme in a brand new tempo and rhythm, and in the bright major key. The movement then winds up in a brilliant series of new and humorous little phrases.

Despite the versatility of the rondo style, it was not always the right thing in the right place. This explains why we find so many varieties of designs in the finales of sonata structures, ranging from the playful rondo tunes of Haydn to the gigantic architecture of the finale of Beethoven's *Ninth Symphony* that culminates in the stupendous orchestral and choral variations based on the noble conception of universal brotherhood.

Treading in the footsteps of Beethoven, Brahms was also an unflinching seeker of dramatic truth, and the creator of sonata forms that demonstrate absolute music at its loftiest. He, too, found that such ideals posed constant problems that admitted almost as many solutions as the number of works in which they arose. The final movement of his *Fourth Symphony* is unique in form and among the rarest things in music—a tragic ending whose magnificence can be fully appreciated only in the light and sound of the first three movements and the problems they presented.

Brahms had written a powerful and intense first movement, a lyrical but majestic and significant second movement, and an exhilarating third movement—a rondo, incidentally—which ended triumphantly but did not have quite enough weight or finality because it was too short, too terse. Moreover, it was not in the home key. What to do? This was the identical question that Tchaikovsky also had to answer in his *Pathétique Symphony*. Both composers concluded that only the spirit of tragedy could bring validity to their works. But their solutions were very different. Tchaikovsky was a melancholy romantic who solved his problem in the structural simplicity of a first-movement sonata form without the development section, and in a mood of utter despair, beginning with this anguished theme. 118

Brahms, on the other hand, was the courageous classicist whose hero also had to die, but die unflinchingly and gloriously. Brahms therefore avoided any semblance of the structural complexity so richly exploited in the previous movements. Instead, he wrote a passacaglia, whose dignified pace and character lent itself inevitably and perfectly to development through a series of variations.

Some of the finest sets of variations ever written and some of the finest fugues, too, are to be found in last movements of the sonata forms, and for excellent reasons. Nothing is easier to follow than a straightforward melody, embellished in a variety of ways with increasing brilliance. Even in the subtler and deeper types of variations, where the melody is disguised by a completely different exterior, we can follow its action much as we do a character in a play who reappears each time in a new costume. Variations and fugues both attain effective climaxes through a cumulative momentum, and both solve the problem of expanding the length of instrumental pieces without the incumbrances of the features of the more dramatic sonata forms.

Small wonder then that the variation form enjoyed so much favor with composers who sought some clear, contrasting design to round out a mighty work importantly. That too accounts for Brahms's choice of a passacaglia to crown his *Fourth Symphony*. Brahms's majestic theme rides on top of a rising series of chords, strikingly harmonized and richly orchestrated. In the first variation, the theme and chords are retained exactly, but in a lower register, and sharply syncopated. In variation two, the theme is below, and a melody in the woodwinds rises above it. In variation three, the melody is again on top, boldly restated. In variation four, the theme is now in the bass as the violins take up a flowing and animated melody and the woodwinds introduce counter-rhythms. 🎵 119

And so on, through thirty marvelous variations that provide incredible contrast through their unexpected harmony, texture, rhythm, and orchestration, and also through constantly shifting moods and dramatic effects, from plaintive whisperings to volcanic climaxes. The theme is always present, but sometimes so delicately hidden that we will only spoil our pleasure and miss Brahms's intention completely if we start to hunt for it. When you hear this great work from beginning to end, you will notice that the variations are in one key—mostly minor, sometimes major. So Brahms adds a coda in which he compresses his theme and modulates daringly through fresh harmonies to a proud and solemn conclusion.

Although Brahms alone insisted constantly that he "stood in the shadow of Beethoven," musical literature teems with the evidence that with few exceptions it was no more possible for any symphonic composer to evade the master's influence than to escape the forces of nature. In one of Beethoven's earliest works, his unique power or organization asserted itself to create a new device that had important consequences. You will remember the rondo theme in the last movement of Beethoven's *Pathétique Sonata for Piano*. 🎵 120

This theme derives straight out of the first movement. 🎵 121

We also called to attention how, in his *Fifth Symphony,* Beethoven effected a direct connective relationship by making the theme of his scherzo reappear in the last movement. But his most far-reaching innovation through this device occurs in the introduction to the last movement of his *Ninth Symphony,* where he quotes themes from the previous three movements. Dramatically, his object is clear: First, he reminds us briefly of the other movements only to reject them as inadequate to express the ideal joy he has in mind, which appears in a new theme finally and exultantly hymned by human voices.

In the process, Beethoven not only created a dramatic milestone, but also a powerful new means of attaining musical unification. This gave rise to whole schools of composition and to the term "cyclic form," to describe symphonies that use the same themes as unifying agents through various movements. This fascinating fabric of thematic links inevitably challenged some composers to see how much they could make out of one theme, or out of only a few, by transforming them into all sorts of different themes.

The transformation of a theme, by itself, is no great trick. Turning a slow theme into a fast theme, or vice versa, or reharmonizing it, or turning it upside down, does not take much poetic imagination. It's not even clever—because anything will lend itself to such devices. Mechanical methods of thematic development, by themselves, have very little to do with musical logic or continuity. What does matter is the inherent character and potentiality of a theme and the effect that its future appearance has on the architecture and momentum of a large structure.

The music of Liszt, which attempts to carry to the *nth* degree the innovation of deriving material from a single thematic cell, shows that the mere transformation of themes, no matter how ingeniously devised, can no more achieve a sense of movement or construct a work of inexorable power, such as a Beethoven symphony or a Wagner opera, than spires, belfries, and stained-glass windows, piled one upon the other, would inevitably guarantee the construction of a great cathedral.

Perhaps the most successful and significant symphonic work in the cyclic form is the justly famous *Symphony in D Minor* by César Franck. As a church organist, Franck developed a marvelously improvisational style, which lent itself perfectly to the leisurely transformation of ideas. In his great symphony, each idea emerges with its own vitality and individuality, not as a disguised spirit from former movements clutched at in desperation by a composer whose inspiration is waning. Here are a few illustrations of Franck's masterly manipulation of his material. The symphony begins with a group of slow themes. ◆ 122

Soon, Franck uses the initial theme to commence the vigorous first movement. ◆ 123

Several pregnant themes are announced in the first movement. Here is a particularly exhilarating one. ◆ 124

And here is a beautiful tune played on the English horn, heard early in the second movement. ◆ 125

Although the finale is full of new and wonderful ideas of its own, do not allow them to blot out the memory of former themes, for their recurrence, in masterful transformation, is the crux of Franck's handling of the cyclic form. The introduction explains the relationship between the key of the previous movement and this one, leading to a festive new theme. ◆ 126

Remember that plaintive second-movement theme for the English horn? Listen to how grand it has become. ◆ 127

When the extraordinarily massive coda begins, you will meet old friends from former movements in more somber moods. At the return to the home key other previous themes emerge in new ways and new relationships, and at the triumphant end of the movement Franck treats his main theme in the same manner as we illustrated "Frère Jacques"—as "a canon at two bars," should its technical term be of interest. ◆ 128

THE CONCERTO

Before leaving this discussion of instrumental forms that employ the large sonata structures, we should delineate the particular features that distinguish a concerto from a sonata.

In the uniquely striving nature of the concerto, from its earliest appearance in the sixteenth century to so dissimilar an example as Shostakovich's perky *Concertino for Two Pianos,* the style never fails to emphasize one primary feature: the age-old opposition between unequal forces. The simplest musical prototype of the concertos of our concert repertory was the seventeenth-century vocal aria with orchestra. No development in art was more inevitable. The human voice is not alone the oldest and most beautiful of "instruments," but as soon as it is heard it has the personality to push instrumental combinations into the background, especially aided by the power of words to command attention. However, unless special provision is made, the sheer volume and weight of an orchestral group could easily frustrate the vocal soloist striving not only to penetrate through it impressively, but even to dominate it. This is even truer of the instrumental soloist, and it will account for the fact that though the solo concerto was already thoroughly established in the time of Bach and Handel, its maturity as an ideal dramatic medium had to await the rise of the sonata and its masters, the extended range and enrichment of the orchestra and its instruments, and the greater proficiency of instrumentalists.

At the outset, an art form had to be devised, one which would enable a composer to capitalize on a rich orchestra without swamping the soloist, and would also enable the soloist to stand out against an orchestra that had acquired formidable color, contrast, and independence.

This was the nub of the problem that fascinated and challenged so many composers and which opened the possibilities of a great many different solutions—almost as many as there are concertos. Nevertheless, all successful examples will be found to have one distinctive feature in common: They will all revel precisely in the disparity between the solo and the orchestra by making it a special point of expressivity, by allocating to each what it can do best by its very nature. It immediately became obvious that a solo instrument (the individual) has the natural advantages of personal magnetism and facile mobility, but cannot compete with an orchestra (the crowd) in climactic force.

The classical solution that enabled both elements to realize their greatest potentialities was to let the orchestra begin with a significant musical paragraph that introduced all or most of the material. In this way it enters significantly without being repressed, as it would be were it to act merely as a supporting accompaniment to the solo. However, it should not have the self-sufficient character of a symphony opening because it has a totally different function—to create expectation for the dramatic entrance of the main character, the soloist. Otherwise, the arrival of the soloist would sound like an intrusion.

In the classical concerto, therefore, the soloist's entrance is calculated to attract even more attention than the crowd, as the well-placed individual can always do on the stage or in life itself. After the soloist has firmly asserted himself, either with the materials of the orchestral introduction or with new material to be combined with it, he then enters into a discussion with the orchestra as they travel widely together in a circle of keys. After this long adventure, for there is no more spacious design in music than the first movement of a concerto, the time comes for a return home; but the event must be a return brilliant enough to top so exciting a journey.

This poses a knotty question. What kind of momentous climax can be attained by a soloist who must continue to dominate, yet to enlist the cooperation of an orchestra that cannot assert itself fully without drowning him out? The classical answer reveals that one more aspect of the concerto style was rooted in human experience, and also that the solo concerto flowered in an age of extemporization. Having now reached a point of reconciliation, the crowd is eager to hear a summation of the situation by the individual who has won its respectful attention. It pauses, while he orates. This, of course, is our familiar friend the cadenza, another holdover from the Baroque aria in which the singer always extemporized a flourish while the orchestra waited silently for the moment of reunion which would end the piece.

The same device, only far more elaborate, appeared in the first movement of concertos when the soloist, usually the composer, improvised a cadenza on the spot. At its climax, poised at the edge of the home key, the orchestra, long pent up, now bursts in and repeats triumphantly in the home key an appropriate theme that has not been heard since the soloist's first entry, and which brings the work to a victorious conclusion.

We can readily recognize the early incorporation of the new sonata plan, with its three main divisions, into the concerto structure. The effectiveness and appeal of the solo concerto made it the major musical entertainment of the eighteenth century, and its popularity persists today. But the classical layout exists in no more than a few dozen concertos, most of them by Mozart; and it will lead to nothing but confusion if we try to find this scheme among the post-classical concertos that have become public favorites. Nevertheless, one or more of its basic principles pertain to every concerto, no matter how much it may depart from the classical scheme: All concertos owe most of their vitality to the initial opposition and final harmonious reconciliation between uneven forces. This applies no less to the poignant slow movements of Bach's concertos, than to the sensational sparklers of Liszt and Paganini, Saint-Saëns and Tchaikovsky, and Rachmaninoff and Prokofiev, none of whom could resist the spectacular possibilities of a flaming orchestra combined with a whiz-bang virtuoso.

We also find in the concerto literature some of the deepest profundities of Mozart, Beethoven, and Brahms. In Beethoven's *Fourth Piano Concerto,* for example, he lets the soloist announce the first phrase, and then lets the orchestra enter quietly with the same phrase in a faraway key. ◗ 129

Immediately after this intense moment, the orchestra sets the stage with a whole procession of themes. Then the piano re-enters to join the orchestra with extraordinary improvisational freedom, introducing new themes and developing old ones in the most beautifully surprising and dramatic ways. Throughout the three miraculous movements, both Beethoven and the concerto style reach new heights.

And if we search high and low for a concerto opening that shows a more startling contrast to Beethoven's *Fourth Piano Concerto,* we find it in his *Fifth Concerto,* which anyone who knows its history and Beethoven's disillusionment with Napoleon will desist from calling the "Emperor." Notice the sharp contrast between the initial statements of the *Fourth* and *Fifth Concertos.* Instead of a soft introduction, there is a majestic pronouncement. Instead of the piano starting alone, the piano and orchestra start together. Instead of a harmonic surprise, there is the strongest assertion of the home key. Instead of a formalized theme, there is a rhapsodic outburst. 130

And now, after all these innovations, the orchestra alone launches on the significant section that we come to expect in a classical concerto. But this one is especially spacious, and, when you hear the concerto in its entirely, do not be surprised to find at least five distinct themes plus any number of important fragments, which Beethoven develops and expands importantly. And do not fail to enjoy the orchestral coloring that is as rich as the harmonic adventure, and the moods that vary from hushed and mysterious quiet to the fury of hailstorms.

In this movement, we reach another milestone in musical history. One of the conventions that Beethoven inherited was that moment in the first movement of concertos when the orchestra pauses and the soloist extemporizes a cadenza. Until the turn of the nineteenth century, the concerto soloist was almost invariably the composer, whose gift for extemporizing was highly developed, and of special interest to the audience. The rise of the performer, already in Beethoven's time, posed a new problem. The virtuoso was not necessarily an improviser or a composer, and the custom of trusting him to fill up the blank tastefully, even adequately, became dangerous. Or so we can assume, for in this concerto, Beethoven forebade and prevented any improvisation—for the first time in musical history—by composing his own cadenza and incorporating it into the actual score.

Beethoven thereby pointed the way to the modern concerto style, though it was Mendelssohn who actually established it—most notably in his unsurpassed *Violin Concerto*. Its very first movement broke instantly with classical concerto style by eliminating the purely orchestral statement of its material, and by the startling placement of the cadenza before the recapitulation. There are the usual three movements, but Mendelssohn initiated a structural stroke of originality by linking them together by the subtlest means. This wonderful work actually aided the stature of concerto writing at a crucial time, when it was being corrupted by a spate of empty display pieces. When Mendelssohn's *Violin Concerto* appeared, it was termed "Greek" in its purity and compression, despite the newness of its architectural features. The concerto opens with the soloist asserting himself immediately in the full statement of his theme, accompanied by the orchestra. ⏺ 131

The orchestra soon asserts itself by breaking in with a theme of its own, initiating a dramatic discussion. An exquisite and historic moment occurs at the energetic end of the first movement. Instead of terminating the movement, Mendelssohn effected a subtle transition of the highest imaginative force, which changes the key and mood and leads directly into the lovely second movement. The illustration demonstrates those few measures that rarely are heard at public performances because of the bursts of applause that greet the last loud chord and obliterate the poetic bridge that emerges from it and connects the first and second movements. ⏺ 132

The wistful slow movement continues in its course until it,

too, is connected to the happy and zestful finale of a prophetic concerto that ranks first in the estimation and affection of most violinists. Although the public's concern is artistic results rather than technical processes, its enthusiasm for this work is inescapably enhanced by the flawlessness of Mendelssohn's mastery in producing a new art form based on the universal principles of the concerto style.

The receptivity of ninteenth-century music lovers to new works and to new performing personalities stimulated composers to the feverish production of works in the concerto style. Structurally, they ranged from the contracted, one-movement forms of Weber's *Konzertstücke,* Schumann's *Fantasie* (which later became the first movement of his piano concerto), Liszt's *Todtentanz* and *Hungarian Fantasia,* and Richard Strauss's *Burleske,* to the expanded, symphonically proportioned concertos of Brahms.

Our century has continued to produce numerous and sharply contrasting concertos. However, whenever we hear a work for one or more solo instruments and orchestra, or even a purely orchestral revival of the old concerto grosso style, no matter how modified, we can assume that regardless of its title, size, or shape, it is based on traditional concerto principles, whose irresistible appeal has never diminished.

Program Music—Instrumentation—Nationalism

Characteristics that are no less prominent in musical art than in life are not found only in the concerto style. The power of suggestion is common to both normal life and to normal art, and it plays a leading role in program music—the instrumental music that illustrates something outside of itself.

Musical symbolism is very old, because musical sound is so strongly suggestive of human emotions, from serenity to fury, and also of the sounds and moods inspired by nature—by the whistling of the wind, by a sunset, or by a thunderclap. But musical description is even older than symbolism, because the earliest music was vocal, and until recently vocal music was invariably accompanied by words, and words are inevitably associative. Although program music is derived from these ancient sources, we use the term rigidly to mean instrumental music without words which describes nonmusical ideas.

In this connotation, program music is the child of Berlioz and Liszt, whose tonal transcriptions of literary and pictorial events became so vital a part of Romanticism. Program music also became so popular a style that it tended more and more to crowd absolute music off symphonic programs. This is quite natural, for everyone loves a story. Yet music has no real ability to relate anything specific, and when a composer decides to tell some story in music, he is compelled to tell it to us also in words. This can lead to some curious situations. Nothing is more ludicrous than the sight of concertgoers, noses buried in program notes, trying to follow the exact details of an elaborate narrative while a piece of program music is being played. Obviously, their attention is not centered on the music, and the same can be said of any composer who becomes more concerned with chronological and realistic details than with the inherent artistic dictates of his musical material.

A composer may be literary, as Tovey remarked, but he has no business being literal. Music is a language of its own, able to express precisely what words cannot express, and its uniqueness lies exactly in its untranslatability. Music has its own inexorable laws, its own necessities of structure and proportion. The ability of a piece of descriptive music to live and to survive depends entirely on how it stands up as music—not on how literally it follows its subject.

Strangely enough, it was Beethoven, the arch-master of absolute music, who, with fantastic foresight, summed up once and for all the theory of program music when he said that works such as his *Pathétique* and *Appassionata* sonatas, the *Pastorale* and *Eroica* symphonies, were "the expression of feeling rather than tone painting." And it was Schumann, the arch-Romanticist, who confessed that he invented most of his titles after the compositions were completed. These statements alone should be quite enough to make us realize that the greatest works of program music are not what they are because they most faithfully fit the ideas they are supposed to illustrate, but because they are masterpieces of design and movement, whose dramatic intentions lent themselves, perhaps generally, but admirably, to musical organization, integration, and pictorial instrumentation.

The development of program music went hand in hand with the development of the orchestra, and of instrumentation, which enabled composers to attain new heights of brilliance and color. Instrumentation deals with the tonal timbre and technical possibilities of instruments and voices. Our century describes this art as "orchestration," because we live in an orchestral age that has witnessed the culmination of a century and a half of musical history during which the technical perfection of musical instruments resulted in a versatility and beauty of instrumental sound that has made orchestration one of the most popular branches of musical art.

Just as human voices have individual physical characteristics, so have instruments. There was, therefore, never a time, and hardly ever an instance, when composers did not conceive their music in the specific medium best suited to the presentation of their ideas.

When we hear a Gregorian chant sung by unaccompanied voices, a Chopin nocturne for piano, an organ fugue by Bach, a Vivaldi concerto grosso for strings, a Sousa march for band, or a Stravinsky ballet scored for our gorgeous and gargantuan orchestras of today, we realize that each period and each style has its own proper sound as well as setting, and that this characterizes it no less importantly than any other of its elements. This is the reason I have suggested from time to time that we may well notice the physical sounds of musical illustrations quite apart from their other aspects.

The orchestral textures of Bach and Handel are woven into solid patterns, without any attempt to blend the different families of sounds represented by the strings, woodwinds, or brasses. Undoubtedly, you are also aware that each movement of these Baroque composers has its own specific instrumental texture and scheme, which do not change during the progress of that movement. What remains to be observed is that the development of dramatic musical expression in the subsequent sonata style was accompanied by a dramatic handling of instrumentation, already so enlarged and expanded by Beethoven that his resources sufficed for Brahms, two generations later.

They even sufficed, with the addition of a few instruments, for Wagner's colossal canvases, despite his awareness of the new orchestral tendencies of his younger contemporary, Hector Berlioz. This inventive genius was forcefully exhibiting instrumental innovations that led directly to our modern orchestration. The evolution of modern orchestration brought still new splendors of sonority and variety and flexibility to each section of the orchestras, and an inexhaustible range of color and brilliance to the entire body. But of even greater importance was its stimulation of new harmonic ideas, as in the magical scores of Debussy, Strauss, and Stravinsky. Once again we see how all the elements of music are inextricably interdependent, how the rise of program music coincided with the development and popularity of the orchestra itself, and so led to new harmonic vistas.

For our purposes, a consideration of instrumentation may conveniently start with Berlioz, for regardless of conflicting opinions about him as a composer, he made a monumental contribution, not only to the development of symphonic opulence, but also to the development of the modern orchestral tone poem. He made the first systematic study of a gigantic orchestra, and completely revolutionized the classical tradition of treating each section as a separate choir. Berlioz' methods blended and mixed the woodwinds and brasses, the percussion and string of the orchestra, exactly as the colors of a sunset are blended. And he accomplished these innovations with a molten imagination, and the most adroit technique. All this is demonstrable in the recorded illustration of the concluding section of Berlioz' "Roman Carnival Overture." I picked this excerpt from the second act of his opera *Benvenuto Cellini* as a pointed reminder that Berlioz was also the man who took dramatic music out of the opera house and put it into the concert hall. Incidentally, this was sheer expediency, owing to the difficulties he experienced in trying to break into the theatre.   ⬤ 133

Chronologically after Berlioz, Rimsky-Korsakov was the next master of both descriptive music and orchestration. There is poetic justice in the fact that the author of the greatest treatise on instrumentation was also an unexcelled master of that art. Rimsky-Korsakov's imagination was also fired by fairy tales and luminous literary landscapes. Such a rhapsodist was bound to become almost exclusively the composer of stage music and program music—all of it full of the gorgeous color and rich fantasy that one finds in picture books. Rimsky-Korsakov taught that instrumentation is the very soul of an orchestral composition, that a work should be conceived orchestrally from its very inception, and that it is no more possible to separate music from its orchestration than it is to separate painting from its colors.

In discussing his own "Scheherazade" suite, he also insisted, "Stories and pictures help some of us to find our themes. But themes are purely musical matters to be developed according to their own artistic integrity and demands. Let us and our audiences release ourselves, however, from the absurdities of sequential realism—indeed, from realism at all." This was evidently a sideswipe at Liszt's tone poems, whose themes and forms were mechanically manipulated to fit the chronological sequence of their stories. Nevertheless, Rimsky-Korsakov himself was no stranger to realism, when he felt it was the right thing in the right place. In the last movement of "Scheherazade," for example, his imagination was equal to a magnificent delineation of a wild festival aboard a ship that, in the midst of the orgy, strikes a magnetic rock and is doomed—a section that also serves as an example of this artist's fabulous orchestral powers. 134

The flamboyant scores of Berlioz and Rimsky-Korsakov influenced almost every subsequent master of program music—even that most unlikely candidate, the most subtle and sensuous of all tone painters, Claude Debussy. But Debussy, as we know, was always a ceaseless searcher for subtle color, and never was he more successful, nowhere did he exercise his incredible imagination and skill more surely in blending conflicting moods and instrumental tints, than in his program music, never so graphically as in his orchestral masterpiece *La Mer*. In this music, there are the rarest harmonies, with shifting, iridescent plays of light and shade, and there is also gentleness and violence. But no matter what the mood, this music is remarkably suggestive of the indefinable mysteries of the sea, a sea of fantasy dreamt by a visionary mystic.

Now we must also return to Richard Strauss as a master of masters among program-music composers and orchestrators. Many of his wild-eyed disciples, not content with the musical quotations that represent characters or moods in Strauss's programmatic tone poems, have invented blow-by-blow analyses in which one is given elaborate, precise interpretations of practically every measure. How, for example, in the tone poem *Don Juan,* this measure represents the Don's passion; that one represents his pursuit of a maiden's grandmother, and so on. And no one, not even Rimsky-Korsakov, ever got more amusement out of such play-by-play descriptions than Strauss himself. For he had a delightful sense of humor, and on more than one occasion made sly, and even vicious, remarks about his pretentious disciples. He could well afford that, for most of Strauss's famous tone poems do not depend at all upon literal symbolism. They stand up as convincing masterpieces of music, without the aid of any program notes whatsoever. Instead of trying to follow the specific story of *Don Juan,* give yourself to the moods that inspired Strauss. Then, when you get the chance to hear the whole piece, you will instinctively feel the rightness of its form. You will have no trouble in responding to its large emotional issues—the fiery ardor of Strauss's hero; the charm of women; and finally, the idealist's disillusionment and partial atonement through death. That is the general idea behind the music meant to express the glorious passion of Dan Juan. You will recall from Illustration 62 how the exciting opening instantly flashes a candid camera shot of the youthful vigor and exultation of the Don. Now let's hear graphically, how Don Juan's death in a duel is implied by mournful fragments of formerly powerful themes—the music rising again to a momentary climax in revival of youthful and heroic memories. ➡ 135

The rise of program music also and inevitably inspired the

development of the elaborately choreographed story ballet. For sheer make-believe musical enchantment, without benefit of stage props and choreography, nothing has surpassed the orchestral suite extracted from Tchaikovsky's ballet *The Nutcracker*. The scene, of course, is a Christmas-tree party, where there are not only children, but also dolls that move as if they were alive. The "Dance of the Sugar Plum Fairy" is a revealing example of the many ways in which imagery can inspire a composer. The orchestration includes a celesta, for which Tchaikovsky wrote an important part. He had heard the instrument when he was in Paris, and he wrote to his publisher in Moscow, urging him to buy the instrument, which Tchaikovsky said cost 1,200 francs. "I expect this new instrument will make an enormous impression," he wrote. The result exceeded the composer's expectation. ● 136

I think it is safe to say that if a group of musicians sat around informally and listed what they considered the three greatest symphonic ballets of the last century, which were also great pieces of descriptive music and of orchestration, one work would undoubtedly appear on every list—the ballet *Daphnis and Chloé* by Maurice Ravel. This orchestrally luscious and rhythmically extravagant score has all the elegance of the old French courts with their masques and dances, their kings, queens, and consorts. It also has its own independence of form, its own fascinating, unexpected contrasts, and kaleidoscopic coloration. For exquisite poetry in music, none surpasses the scene of Daphnis lying stretched before the grotto of the nymphs, as the day gradually dawns and the birds sing. The glittering conclusion recalls Isadora Duncan's remark, "To dance is to go mad with the body."

Ravel's subtleties included a Gallic streak of ironic humor and urbane brilliance. Both are exemplified in his most popular ballet and symphonic work, *Bolero*. This sensationally successful composition is admittedly a trick, but one of the most amazing artistic tricks ever performed. Here is the carefully prepared harmonic surprise of the conclusion. ● 137

NATIONALISM

Topical significance did not enter the world of ballet until the twentieth century, but the inspiration for much of the program music composed in the nineteenth century derived directly from the political and social upheaval that culminated in a torrential stream of nationalism and overflowed all the arts. In music, nationalism became an inseparable part of the entire Romantic movement and helped to shape musical composition in virtually every form. Its intensive sentiments were evident in Chopin's utilization of Polish dance rhythms, in the Magyar rhapsodies of Liszt, in the Czech spirit and sound of Smetana and Dvořák, in Wagner's operatic glorification of the Rhineland, and in numerous other works.

In powerful, triumphant countries, composers could express patriotic pride, as Tchaikovsky did by writing the *1812 Overture,* in celebration of the great Russian victory of that year. In the weaker, subjected nations, composers could express aspiration for liberation in stirring music based on native melodies and rhythms. Song writers could inspire and justify their compatriots by setting the lyrics of some nationally beloved poet, living or dead, to impassioned music. Symphonic and operatic composers could base tone poems and operas on national heroes, on native sagas, on events past and present, legendary and historical.

The musical roots of nationalism are truly grass roots reaching deep into the soil and the soul of the country and its common people, the folk. It is folk music that is the genesis and apotheosis of national music, for without the folk element, the national character is lost. This folk element may show itself in many different ways. The composers of art-music have been consciously using folk music since the early nineteenth century, but for the most part they have tended to employ it as a special entity, rather than to integrate it into their own styles.

There are three major ways in which a composer can make use of folk material. First, he can merely harmonize an actual folk song, either in a way that emphasizes the folk style or in a way designed to bring the song into closer conformity with the prevailing standards of art-music. Béla Bartók's folk-song settings are typical of the former, while Beethoven's Irish, Scottish, and Welsh songs reflect the latter approach. Second, a composer may change folk melodies to conform to harmonic, instrumental, and/or rhythmic demands that differ greatly from the traditions that gave rise to the original material, as in MacDowell's *Indian Suite*. Finally, a composer may create an imitative folk style of his own and if, as a result, he acquires renown as a "folk composer," it is usually because long exposure to, or musicological study of a particular folk idiom, has caused him to become saturated with its intrinsic style and feeling.

Nationalism compels our return to Antonin Dvořák—a towering figure and a mighty master among the great orchestral composers—who accepted with pride his reputation as a rustic genius and who remained a "primitive" in style and spirit in virtually all his works. Saved from a butcher's fate by his prodigious musical talent, Dvořák nonetheless clung close to the soil all his life. His musical genius first bore fruit when, in his early thirties, he emerged from his initial eclectic flounderings to respond to the Czech spirit that was his true nature, and that had utterly permeated his musical soul. From then on, in all the musical forms he essayed, the stamp was most emphatically Czech and double-Czech. However, his was no narrow nationalism. It was representative of a broad Slavic sensitivity that reached from his native Bohemia to all Slavic communities, whether in Moravia, Silesia, Slovakia, Ruthenia, or Poland. Nowhere is this more evident than in his *Slavonic Dances,* in which he incorporated all the musical elements from all these backgrounds. His *Eighth Slavonic Dance* furnishes an excellent example of his intrinsic Czech spirit. ◖ 138

Dvořák's ear was so attuned to indigenous folk characteristics that when he came to the United States in the 1890's he was able to absorb the melodic and rhythmic essence of both the American and the American-Negro idioms into his music; furthermore, he captured their ethnic associations of the melodies, and presented them in eminently Czechoslovakian works—without in any way disturbing the stylistic quality of the music. The most familiar case is the famous "Goin' Home" segment of the *New World Symphony,* our Illustration 111, inspired by Negro tradition.

The three years of Dvořák's activities in the United States, as a great nationalist composer and also as a pedagogue, proved extremely profitable to us as well as to him. Apart from producing his most popular symphony and a fine chamber-music work entitled "The American Quartet," Dvořák brought home to North American composers the need and potentiality for freeing themselves from European tradition, and for creating an indigenous national art. The ideal did not materialize until the twentieth century, but it would be remiss not to acknowledge Dvořák's potent influence upon its realization.

In South America during the first half of our century, a genuine nationalism arose in a vast body of over two thousand works that represent the pungent and cultivated art of the Brazilian composer Heitor Villa-Lobos. This intensely patriotic and imaginative creator once asked, "Do you want to know what folklore is? Well," he continued, answering himself, "I am folklore." And what he meant was that nationalism in music goes much deeper than the quotation of folk melodies or dances conceived long ago. When we hear the music of composers like Villa-Lobos and Dvořák, whose roots strike deep into their soils, we are hearing folklore of a sort. But it is very hard to tell which melodies are borrowed and which are composed.

The same can be said about Jean Sibelius, who was not only a major creator but also a heroic symbol of his country. His art brought enormous interest and respect to Finland. It is as difficult to explain as it is impossible to deny, that every note Sibelius composed belongs to the culture, climate, and soil of his native Finland. Yet Sibelius never used one measure of music that was not of his own invention. I hasten to assure you that I am not forgetting the famous chorale from *Finlandia,* which was set to words and adopted as a national patriotic song. Universally and mistakenly, it is regarded as a "national anthem"—and that is not too far from wrong, as we can hear in a brief excerpt from the concluding section. 139

Sibelius is Finnish in exactly the way that Wagner is German; Debussy, French; Johann Strauss, Austrian; Elgar, British; and Gershwin, American. Gustav Mahler once said that Sibelius had already composed the mountains of his homeland. Sibelius' career began and ended with tone poems. In between, everything that he wrote stamped him as a master craftsman. Even those who belittle him do not deny that at all times he was a simple artist whose love for the elemental, for the fields and the forests, for water and mountain, for legend and natural phenomena, are eloquently reflected in numerous symphonies and tone poems— music made of familiar elements, yet sounding like nothing ever written before or since.

Although the love and glorification of homeland reflected the fondest feelings and hopes of millions of people, nationalism eventually succumbed to a shrinking globe, and composers began to fall under the spell of cultures other than their own. All of us know the attraction that opposites have for each other, the glamor that distance has for all of us, and the conviction that the other fellow's grass is always greener. These basic emotions found expression in many works by German, French, and Russian composers, particularly those who found inspiration in the cultures of Italy and Spain, Scotland, the Orient, and other distant places.

When we heard Rimsky-Korsakov's *Scheherazade,* we were hearing a work inspired by an Asiatic fairy tale. The Frenchman

Bizet found his inspiration for *Carmen* in the warmth and color of Spain. Mendelssohn wrote an *Italian* and a *Scotch* Symphony. Verdi's *Aida* evoked the splendor of ancient Egypt, and Puccini's *Madame Butterfly* was set in the exotic Far East.

These works represent some of the culminating achievements of a period of nationalistic fervor that literally burst its boundaries and then began to disappear when, with Debussy, Rimsky-Korsakov, Richard Strauss, and Ravel, we move into the twentieth century. It should aid musical understanding to notice that, despite the striking individuality of each of these composers, all of their works demonstrate the continuity of art. Even though as creators these men represented widely differing idioms, styles, methods, and habits, their music emerges as the inventive expansion of recognizable traditions that remained unbroken, whether seen in the Classicism of Dvořák, the Romanticism of Rimsky-Korsakov, the Impressionism of Debussy and Ravel, the Expressionism of Richard Strauss, or the Elementalism of Sibelius.

But such fixed terms become nuisances. Within each period, within each style, these composers and numerous others throughout history, were producing works of the strongest contrasts and of overlapping categories that defy any classification. In this age of instant communication, in this world that has become one world so far as art is concerned, we must not forget that the development of Western art-music was for a long time the work of a comparatively small number of nations; that others were either slowly awakening from a very long sleep, or, like America, were just emerging from artistic infancy.

Understandably, at the turn of the century, despite the presence of such excellent American composers as MacDowell, Horatio Parker, and John Knowles Paine, our art-music showed little trace of anything specifically nationalistic. There was but one prophetic native voice among our composers—Charles Ives—who was imbued with the ideas and ideals of Emerson, Hawthorne, and Thoreau, and who attempted to create the music of their common New England heritage. Ives was a bold and unconventional spirit, but his prophetic achievements were extremely complex and uneven, and remained unnoticed until quite recently.

Consequently, in the early decades of this century, the American spirit was to be found mainly in the ballads of Stephen Foster and in the stirring marches of John Philip Sousa. But marvelous as they are, they are not within the domain of our primary concern—the significant symphonic works of musical literature. Until the advent of the twentieth century, this literature was rooted in Europe. Since then, forces have been at work that within less than half a century have made our country an international musical center teeming with creative, interpretative, and educational activities of the highest standards. Modern means of communication have made music available to every American child and adult.

The quality and quantity, the magnitude and depth, of musical activity and musical interest in the United States are observable in every phase of the contemporary scene.

The Contemporary Musical Scene

From the inception of the twentieth century, the world has been in the throes of turbulent change. That in itself is not unduly remarkable, for change is the unchanging characteristic of every aspect of life and history. What distinguishes our century is the bewildering speed and violence with which changes have occurred; the way in which evolution has assumed the pace of revolution.

Music, as a living language, constantly changes, and always has —sometimes gradually and sometimes rapidly. Curiously, our century's frontal attack on tradition is the least modern aspect of musical modernism. In 1300, and again in 1600, music witnessed volcanic explosions when the established art was attacked by composers who felt that it had come to a dead end, that the only way to attain new means of expression was to pursue entirely new paths. In our time, at the equidistant point of 300 years, history repeated itself.

What differentiated the 1900 upheaval was the totality of its attack—not only on the esthetic ideals, but also on the essential elements of music. And it also reversed the more usual chronological sequence of events followed by art that interprets them, for instead of reflecting our era's uprooted social, political, and economic structures, the musical manifestation actually anticipated these eruptions a full decade before World War I. But wherever art stands in relation to the march of other human events, it has always been considerably more than the mere reflection of the spirit of its age. If there has ever been any such thing as "the spirit of an age," which was inevitably expressed in one prevailing artistic policy or practice, in one technique or style only, it was certainly not in music. And this may account for some of the mischief caused by the very term "modern music."

We will understand modern music and each other far better if we agree immediately to define modernism as "of our time" or "of recent period"—denoting music that reflects a wide range of accomplishment and endeavor, from the conservative to the radical, from the inspired to the contrived, and from the masterful to the meretricious. Then, if we will also agree to call only that part of it which is in total revolt against the past, "experimental," we will be able to follow better the complicated crosscurrents that swirl about the mainstream of music today.

At first glance, the contemporary musical scene appears to be in a state of hopeless confusion, because we are right on top of it—and in that sense, it is. Never before in musical history has so much of musical history been available, and so instantaneously, to so many. Modern communication techniques have brought virtually the entire musical past into the present, and music of all ages, designed for the ear, can now be appraised by the ear, and not merely studied by the eye. Therefore, the music of our own time is inescapably being heard and evaluated in living relation to all that preceded it and all that surrounds it. Unless the composer of today is to write in a professional vacuum—and not a few have chosen this path—the past continually sounds in his ear, exerting its powerful influence, and yet challenging him to break new ground, to expand his technical and esthetic horizons, to discover new ways of stating old truths.

We have reviewed each musical epoch that preceded us through its towering composers and their notable works. This is precisely the way in which our era will be evaluated by posterity, and precisely the way in which we can begin to evaluate it now. There are many among us who insist that we are just too close to new music to judge it accurately. If that is so, they are saying that our generation is less sensitive and less intelligent than previous generations. Musical history—not that part which passes for history and is actually musical mythology—proves beyond doubt that the collective judgment of average music lovers in every age has correctly anticipated posterity's judgment in intuitive selection of the greatest men and their greatest works. There is no valid reason for thinking that our generation is any less responsive and responsible.

Unless history reverses itself totally, posterity will not consider us unjustified if we evaluate our composers by the identical musical norms and standards which have prevailed for at least four centuries. So let's plunge bravely ahead and illustrate twentieth-century music through what this century's music lovers and critics have generally agreed are the most vital and communicative works of the most important composers—works we not only understand, but love. They stand as monuments of true creative power which have spoken to us so eloquently that we have already accorded them the status of classics. Needless to say, countless other works belong in an important sense to the bewilderingly rich literature of twentieth-century music. But we are not attempting a comprehensive musical history, and should confine ourselves to the music of the composers who have played the most decisive roles. Previously, we have encountered music by such great masters who lived well into our century as Debussy, Richard Strauss, Sibelius, Ravel, and Rimsky-Korsakov. Now permit me to commend to your private investigation many significant symphonic figures whom we have to omit, some of whom bridge the nineteenth and the twentieth centuries and whose destiny it was to sum up methods of preceding periods. Prominent among those we have not met are the Austrians Anton Bruckner and Gustav Mahler, the British Edward Elgar, Frederick Delius, and William Walton, the French Albert Roussel and Vincent D'Indy, the Moravian Leoš Janáček, the Spanish Isaac Albéniz and Manuel de Falla, the Russian Alexander Scriabin, the Hungarian Zoltán Kodály, and the Italian Ottorino Respighi, men of superior stature and stylistic refinement but who wrote dominantly within established traditions that were growing less and less promising for more and more composers.

It may surprise you that I am going to begin our consideration of twentieth-century music with a composer who, though he lived more than four decades in this century, used a musical speech that was rooted in the language of his predecessors, and never veered one inch from the direct line of nineteenth-century Romanticism. But there's method in my madness, so please bear with me and listen for a moment. 140

I am sure you know this composition extremely well, as the conclusion of Rachmaninoff's *Second Piano Concerto* or alas, as "Full Moon and Empty Arms." For over half a century now, Rachmaninoff's music has spoken and continues to speak to an enormous public. Rachmaninoff's world was that of Romanticism. Resisting all the newer trends about him, he continued to follow in Tchaikovsky's footsteps, but with more bite and more freedom in his harmony and rhythm, for he did absorb from his contemporaries what it suited him to absorb. But Rachmaninoff himself broke no fresh ground. His critics have accused his music of not reflecting any tendencies of the twentieth century, and they are right. But few seem to have observed the revealing fact that a great deal of the bold and new music written during the time that Rachmaninoff was composing has completely disappeared, while Rachmaninoff's continues to grow more and more meaningful to more and more people. The point is, that in the process of reiterating old truths, Rachmaninoff's individuality emerged in every measure of his finest music, regardless of the source of its inspiration. And this undoubtedly accounts for its enormous and enduring popularity.

Rachmaninoff's achievement points up dramatically the diversity of music composed since 1900 by a host of composers whose styles reflect the entire range of musical expression, from the traditional to the experimental. Nor is it uncommon to find within the compass of even a single composer's output, styles which differ from one period to another as night from day.

If we are looking for a prime example of a contemporary composer who reacted in one form or another to the quickly changing world about him, none has been more consistently and frequently influenced than Igor Stravinsky—for half a century now, the sovereign figure and most powerful influence of twentieth-century music. It would perhaps be easier to mention the styles that Stravinsky has *not* adopted than those he has, for he has never ceased to be driven by the need to renew himself, almost from work to work. Virtually each composition, or at least some element of it, has been an experiment resulting in varying degrees of success and failure.

Stravinsky's creative power was most consistently and forcefully expressed in three early ballet scores: the romantically conceived *Fire Bird*, the impressionistic *Petrouchka,* and finally, the culminating point of this period of Stravinsky's evolution, the completely mature and developed idiom of *The Rite of Spring*. Two brief illustrations, one from *Fire Bird* and the other from *The Rite of Spring,* dramatically demonstrate the extraordinary range of Stravinsky's emotional palette. ● 141

The historic, violently novel, and barbaric ballet *The Rite of Spring* had the good fortune to incite a riot at its 1913 Paris premiere, and to bring Stravinsky world fame at the age of thirty. Its first performance struck the audience with the fury of an explosion, and precipitated a war between two battling factions —those who were incensed at what they considered a blasphemous destruction of everything they had previously considered as music, and those who were entranced and excited by what they considered a masterful new conception of art—a completely successful reorganization of the tonal universe.

As is often the case, such extremes tend to cancel each other. Contrary to a commonly held belief, the revolutionary *Rite of Spring* became a universal favorite with unprecedented rapidity. Within one year of its scandalous premiere it was again performed in Paris, this time in concert form as an orchestral piece. Enthusiastically acclaimed, it won a complete triumph and established Stravinsky once and for all as the most dominant force in modern music—a position he has sustained to this day.

Such success, however, did not satisfy Stravinsky's ever-searching mind, and he entered upon one phase of composition after another, producing a large number of works that range from the delicious nonsense of his *Circus Polka* "composed for a young Elephant," to the complex and uncommunicative opera *The Rake's Progress,* through the ballet of 1957, *Agon,* to the latest twelve-tone experiments.

As we know, works of Stravinsky's later period have found little favor with the mass public, and even formerly reverent critics throughout the world have often reacted strongly and bitterly. Several decades ago in the London Sunday *Times,* Ernest Newman referred to Stravinsky as "a talented craftsman who used to be a genius." In *Le Figaro* of Paris, Bernard Gavoty, a former Stravinsky worshiper, wrote that "the past twenty-five years of Stravinsky have been nothing but sham." Nevertheless, there is no doubt that whatever Stravinsky writes, whatever style he essays, bears the unmistakable stamp of his very own creativity. Despite what has been called "the dramatic and bitter evidence of the aridity and dry senility of his later works," he remains undoubtedly the outstanding compositional figure of our time.

Next to Stravinsky, the most influential, revolutionary, and challenging musical figure of the twentieth century has been the Viennese composer and theorist Arnold Schönberg, who also started his career as a confirmed romanticist. His earliest works show the strong influence of Wagner, Brahms, Mahler, and Richard Strauss, as can be heard in a brief excerpt from his early work *Transfigured Night.* 142

This post-Wagnerian inspiration, and several other works that followed, convinced Schönberg that he could not escape the insinuating influence of his predecessors. He became preoccupied with the problem of how to be original in his own way, and finally concluded that there was nothing left for him but complete revolt. By abolishing the traditional distinction between consonance and dissonance, by the establishment of a twelve-tone school, Schönberg struck a deathblow to the very basis of music itself—tonality.

The construction that Schönberg offered was the twelve-tone row, a system whereby the notes of the scale are prearranged by the composer in an ordered and fixed sequence from which the entire work necessarily derives. The ground rules do not permit any of the twelve notes that make up the row to be sounded twice until all the eleven others have been heard. This arbitrary device makes it quite impossible to polarize either a melody or a harmony, or to establish a home key—that horizon point so crucial to tonality. One could almost say that *a*tonality was Schönberg's new language.

Schönberg's opus 16 is his earliest exploration of what he termed "the emancipation of the dissonance." It is representative of the pioneering movement that he constructed to give music "a new lease on life." Unfortunately, Schönberg was a more significant theorist than a significant composer. It has been said that he may have shown the way to the promised land, but never entered it himself. Schönberg, together with Stravinsky, undoubtedly opened new paths and influenced not only a generation of composers, but also the very direction that music itself has taken. As pioneers, they altered the language of music, but with a crucial difference—Stravinsky actually produced communicative masterpieces, whereas there is bitter irony lurking behind the fact that of all the compositions by Schönberg, the father of dissonance and atonality, the only ones that have communicated anything to the musical public are his early and derivative works.

Nevertheless, Schönberg's pioneering has had a tremendous effect on the history and direction of music, through the prodigious output of dozens of twelve-tone composers. However, only Anton von Webern and Alban Berg, his two favorite pupils, went on to make impressive marks as composers. But Schönberg's influence on them, though seminal, was limited, for both set out in quite different ways to explore new worlds of their own. This was less true of the veritable army of other disciples, whose debt to Schönberg was virtually complete, and who discovered the hardest way that theorizing is one thing, and composing another. There is a long list of these "voices of the future," who were given repeated hearings, who made news, who were proudly hailed by their clique as prophets of progress—and some no less than a decade ago—who have now attained total oblivion.

By 1950, Schönberg himself was being declared obsolete by the avant-garde. The new apostle was Webern, the pointillistic miniaturist whose incredibly condensed and geometric wisps of sound stimulated a large group of twelve-toners to enter new areas of abstraction. Actually, Webern's works are conspicuous by their absence at most concerts, even of the avant-garde, at the present time, indicating that he has perhaps had his day. However, at this moment his influence appears increasingly evident in the music of many contemporaries who are represented at such special concerts.

The one composer who is generally conceded to have utilized Schönberg's methods in the creation of a full-fledged masterpiece was Berg, in his opera *Wozzeck*. Especially significant was his declaration of artistic independence in this work, for Berg did not hesitate to abandon the tone-row technique whenever dramatic exigencies or musical objectives demanded it. While adapting elements of his master's methods, Berg at the same time pursued a thoroughly personal course. He revived the harmonic principle of alternating dissonance and consonance, and allowed his brilliant and dramatic talent to make free use of any and every device of tonality and form that would serve his purpose. *Wozzeck* is sometimes given in a concert version, but portions of it almost never appear on symphonic programs. Actually, a symphonic excerpt renders a disservice to the inherent power of this work, for in order to be properly appreciated the opera must be seen as well as heard, so wonderfully is the music wedded to the action.

Although a composition such as his opus 6, dedicated to Schönberg, is extraordinarily individual and very listenable indeed like so many of Berg's other works, *Wozzeck* remains in my opinion the one truly great work, the one total masterpiece, that has come directly out of the Schönberg school. Though similar, if hardly numerous, claims have been made on behalf of other twelve-tone writings, even twice the number would still be a disappointing production within a system that has been the main field of composition, and internationally, for over half a century.

This fact is significant enough to justify comment. There is no sacrilege in renouncing the traditions of a man-made art; there is no law in music which says that composers must live forever under the charter of classical tonality. Certainly, every artist is privileged to entertain ideals that may be obtainable only at the expense of breaking some or all of the rules of his art. Such actions become not only a privilege, but a necessity, when the time comes for testing the validity of those ideals.

But abolishing the old is not enough. Something—and something affirmative—must take its place. And the mere creation of a new technique is not necessarily that something. Technique is never an end in itself, but only a means. It is matter, not manner, that causes the average music lover to respond to a work of art, and that, in the final analysis, is the determining issue of public judgment. In all pioneering, there is considerable experimentation. Our sophisticated musical public today is well prepared to accept the most extreme examples tolerantly, but they only respond to it emotionally when experimentation is fired with urgency and passion.

The mature creative artist never starts out with inflexible

propositions and devices. He is too emotionally involved and intellectually engrossed in his work to worry about whether his materials and methods are old or new, and he is far too imaginative to imprison himself within the confines of any system or "ism."

Exactly such an artist was the Hungarian genius Béla Bartók, who was not only one of the towering musical figures, but also one of the great spirits of our century. He postulated no theory or system. Despite the austere and dissonant character of some of his music, he was essentially a traditionalist with inexhaustible vision, profound musicianship, and vast technical resources that he employed with meticulous mastery.

"Only a fool," he once said, "would build in defiance of the past." He believed that in art-music, as well as in the authentic Hungarian folk music which he documented and utilized so widely and enthusiastically, development is a matter of evolution, not revolution. He was rooted in the classical language, and his idol and ideal was Beethoven. Of course, he could not serve any purpose by rewriting Beethoven's music, or by imitating his speech, but the classical influence is evident throughout Bartók —in the precise calculation of his construction, and in his concentrated economy of means. In his orchestral works, Bartók adopted the more modern technique of making instrumental color an expressive partner of every mood.

Stylistically, Bartók's music is many-sided. He synthesized, perhaps, more than he invented. Yet every work of his prolific production is imprinted with genuine individuality. In fact, he developed so forceful a personality that virtually every composer who did not follow either Stravinsky or Schönberg, followed Bartók. This is all the more remarkable, for he advocated no specific procedure, and offered no system. He followed only the urgency of his own prodigious imagination.

As for Bartók's mission to reconcile the folk melodies and dance rhythms of his native Hungary with the sophisticated techniques of the mature development of European art-music, he himself supplied the explanation of his singular success. "The way to reap the benefit of one's ground roots," he said, "is to assimilate the idiom of one's peasant music so fully that one can forget all about it and use it as a mother tongue." That is the philosophy behind everything he wrote, including his orchestral masterpiece, the powerful *Concerto for Orchestra*. The title will not puzzle or mislead us when we remember that concertos without solo instruments were the common commodities of the eighteenth century. Of course, the connotation is quite different now in our century and so is the modern orchestra. But we should be well prepared for the work's tendency to use single orchestral instruments, and even various choirs of instruments, in a soloistic manner, in both competition and cooperation with the full orchestra. 143

While Bartók was excavating Magyar melodies and rhythms, and utilizing them in a series of potent works that revealed him as Hungary's greatest composer, a kindred contemporary spirit was pursuing the identical path in England, to become the towering British symphonist of the twentieth century. Throughout the long and active life of Ralph Vaughan Williams, he so immersed himself in the spirit of English folk music that many of his themes are indistinguishable from actual folk tunes. But here was another international nationalist, and Ralph Vaughan Williams seems to me most remarkable for the multitudinous influences he absorbed right up to the last, not excluding the most experimental modernisms. Like Bartók, he revealed himself to be a worshiper of Beethoven's music and musical philosophy. In writing about his *London Symphony,* he said it must stand or fall, "not as a descriptive work, but as absolute music." If listeners recognize suggestions of the Westminster chimes, or London street cries, or English songs, he said, these are to be considered as associative accidents rather than essentials of the music.

From this world-famous symphony, Ralph Vaughan Williams progressed to a tighter, a more dissonantal, and complex style, which reflected our world and also the composer's fear of the many threats to its actual survival. When he began writing in this way, he was no less disturbed by it than his public. "I don't know myself whether I like it," he said, "but this is what I meant, and this is what I felt." Like all first-class creators, he had to follow his own path and conviction. He developed a completely personal style that owes almost nothing to the music of any other composer. He once made a statement that would have made an ideal epitaph. "Whether my music is good or bad," he said, "it is always honest. And by that I mean that I could not put down on paper a line which I did not first feel in every part of me." The remark is as typical as it is timely in an age of self-conscious and objective modernism. It pertains no less to his most famous composition, "Greensleeves," one of the purest and loveliest examples of twentieth-century music, than to his late *Ninth Symphony*—a prophetic and fascinating experiment in sonority, as illustrated in this excerpt.   144

In the fall of 1918, when I was a teen-age piano student, an eager, gaunt young man with reddish-blond hair, owl eyes, and huge flapping ears was brought to our home by friends. He was about to make his New York debut as a pianist. The introductions were barely over before he ran to the piano without being asked, and began to play some music, obviously his own. It cast an immediate spell over all of us. I remember being fascinated by the strangeness of it, and excited by the vitality of his playing. After he played, he talked, and with equal power, molding each phrase with his huge hands; he grew terribly tense as he confided that he wanted to create an entirely new music. This he did not quite do, but he did create his own music, full of power and individuality; much of it is easily among the finest of our century. His name: Serge Prokofiev.

Prokofiev's career began in pre-Revolutionary Russia, contin-

ued through a sixteen-year sojourn in the Western world—
mainly in New York and Paris—and ended in the severe and
censorial atmosphere of the Soviet Union. Due to his exposure
to a far greater range of influences than any of his Soviet contemporaries, it must have been particularly difficult for him to
swallow the doctrines of Soviet officialdom, which proclaimed
that the main goal of artistic endeavor was the glorification of
the state, and which therefore constituted an appalling infringe-
ment upon the right of an artist to express himself as he sees fit.
Prokofiev did not escape periodic governmental displeasure, but
it did not deter him from creating a large number of consequen-
tial works. We must remember that he returned to Russia volun-
tarily, and the reasons are not too hard to understand. Innately
a romanticist, Prokofiev abhorred the antipoetic and dehumanized abstractions that characterized so much of Western art. Fully
aware that certain restrictions might be placed upon his personal
philosophy and esthetic practices in the Soviet Union, he nevertheless felt this was not too high a price for the protection of an
environment in which the composer enjoys a higher artistic, social, and economic status than anywhere else in the world. At
the very least, there he was sure to find an enthusiastic acceptance
of his strong emotional gifts, as he did, for example, in his *Fifth
Symphony,* dedicated to the spirit of man—and without being
branded a reactionary sentimentalist.

Prokofiev may eventually turn out to be the precursor of the
new Romanticism—twentieth-century style. His early, audacious
piano works—*Diabolic Suggestion, Sarcasms,* and the first concertos—abound in grotesque and jagged harmonies, primitive
rhythms, bitter satire. Yet they also abound in delicious melodies
and harmonies. In *Peter and the Wolf* and the *Classical Symphony* are the quintessence of charm and effortlessness of the
lightest humor and vivacity.

Evaluating his total output, which includes his mature piano
and violin concertos, his crowning symphonic achievements of

the *Fourth, Fifth,* and *Sixth Symphonies,* the astonishing piano sonatas and operas, and the numerous scores for the ballet, theatre, and film, one finds that Prokofiev emerges as still another major creator of our epoch. His sumptuous orchestral color, his surprising harmonic and rhythmic vitality, and the amazing versatility of his style, all stamp him as a supreme and unique personality. Slashing cynicism and savagery characterize his *Scythian Suite* for orchestra, a vivid work that was called Prokofiev's answer to Stravinsky's *Rite of Spring.* In the first movement of his *Third Piano Concerto,* we can hear the immediate disclosure of his Romanticism and vigor.   145

Upon Prokofiev's death, Dmitri Shostakovich became the topmost Soviet composer. Although he is entirely a Soviet product, he has also had to endure official condemnation for indulging in "decadent Western formalism." His reaction is revealed in the subtitle of his *Fifth Symphony:* "A Soviet artist's reply to justified criticism." To what degree this total commitment to Soviet policy has affected the composer's music, one can never know. However, Prokofiev's attitude and achievement, in the face of identical condemnation, makes one question whether greater intellectual freedom and ideological independence could have enhanced Shostakovich's artistic power. From a composer who could produce, at the age of nineteen, one of the finest first symphonies ever written, the rest of his abundant output has been a keen disappointment, displaying a steady diminution of creative force. This has much more to do with Shostakovich's own gifts and development than with Soviet socialism. No official line can successfully extinguish, or even dampen, the fires of genuine creativity. The proof lies in the commanding figure of Prokofiev. Against him, all of his younger Soviet contemporaries emerge as frail followers.

The situation of musicians in the United States is entirely different from what it is in the Soviet Union. Perhaps the greatest contribution America has made to mankind has been its ready offer of asylum to people who have suffered some denial of rights, some curtailment of freedom, or actual persecution in the land of their birth. In the last fifty years, these people have included most of the leading composers of twentieth-century music, who subsequently made their homes here to work among us—Rachmaninoff, Stravinsky, Bartók, Schönberg, Bloch, Hindemith, and still others. Each in his own way has already put his mark on our age, and has contributed importantly to the position of the United States as the musical center of the world. Each has been free to go his own way, free to observe any and all musical languages, to judge them for himself, to reject them, or adopt them.

It was for this rich and stimulating environment, not for any needed political protection, that Ernest Bloch emigrated from Switzerland to become an American citizen. The philosophy and humanism of this man, which were expressed verbally many years ago, never materially changed during his lifetime. "There is something tragic," he said, "in the degree to which music has gradually divorced itself from life, and become an egocentric and artificial thing. Art has now broken with life, and this doubtless explains why the events now afflicting mankind have had so little effect upon music. However, I, for one, do not believe that humanity has finished its march."

Staunch faith and burning conviction have also saturated every measure of Bloch's music. His greatest works were conceived as sacred offerings, rooted on principles that he devoutly believed would continue to endure as long as life and art. Yet, whatever he wrote was entirely fresh, and unmistakably contemporary. His ardent voice speaks to us through the musical sounds of our sophisticated century—but with singular sanity and clarity. Over and above Bloch's materials and techniques, his outstanding characteristics are the spirit of aspiration, the passionate temperament, and the fierce, timeless integrity, which place him squarely among the masters.

Perhaps his most significant work, certainly his most widely known, is the Hebrew rhapsody for cello and orchestra, *Schelomo*. Though he always responded deeply to the eloquent spirit that pulsates through Biblical literature, Block is an original artist, not an archeologist. He never attempted the reconstruction of actual Hebrew melodies, but tried, rather, to translate into music the flavor of the Old Testament. *Schelomo* is a masterpiece of throbbing melodiousness, of exotic themes and harmonies, of fanciful orchestral coloring and contrast. It sounds ancient, tribal, yet everything is Bloch's own, and entirely of our age. Our illustration is a revealing example from *Schelomo*, in which the poetic Biblical orations are uttered, not by a singer, but by a cello with a large range—a voice unbound by the limitations of spoken language. ⬤ 146

One hears little of Bloch's music today. He is a casualty of the antiromantic and antispiritual movement of our time. It has been suggested that the fate of his greatest and most individual works can perhaps best be summed up in the Biblical observation, "They have ears, but they hear not."

Somewhat the same can be said for the music of Paul Hindemith, the German composer whose prolific output was banned by the Nazis on the grounds that it was unbearably modern. Ironically, for the past twenty years it has been less and less in evidence on concert programs, precisely because contemporary interpreters consider it too academic and conventional, and the public considers it too unspectacular compared, for example, to the music of Stravinsky. Nevertheless, Hindemith is a big man of our century who has written trenchant and influential works for every instrument of the orchestra, and for the orchestra itself. The finest of these not only rank with, but have influenced, many of the finest works of our time. In addition, we are indebted to Hindemith for his rationality and stability, for his respect for tradition, and for his insistence that one must first know the rules before one can break them. Throughout Hindemith's clear, spacious structures, he has demonstrated his conviction that tonality is to music what gravity is to our planet. Instead of rejecting tonality, he has expanded its range and enlarged its function. The results are genuine harmonic adventures, not sterile theories.

Although Hindemith's most significant orchestral work is the three-movement symphony extracted from his opera, *Mathias the Painter,* our illustration, the *Concerto for Violin and Orchestra,* represents his more familiar "lean, athletic style." 147

Turning now to our native-born American composers, the question inevitably arises, "Is there an American music?" The fact is that both our naturalized and native-born composers have been writing music in every known style. That is why, in this melting pot, we cannot claim a predominant style of American music. Nevertheless and paradoxically, there is indeed an unmistakable American idiom, which by itself would not be important if not for its salutary evidence in many works that disclose both maturity and mastery. My choice of but three American illustrations is due to the simple fact of circumscribed space. It must not for a moment imply any denigration of the first-rate creative abilities of such native symphonic composers as: Samuel Barber, Elliott Carter, Henry Cowell, Paul Creston, Ross Lee Finney, Howard Hanson, Norman Dello Joio, Roy Harris, Benjamin Lees, Peter Mennin, Walter Piston, William Schuman, Roger Sessions, Harold Shapero, William Grant Still, Virgil Thomson, Edgar Varese, and still others. Another album would be needed to consider their work adequately; it is among my plans and hopes.

In any event, first billing belongs to Aaron Copland, who is accepted as the indisputable dean of American musical composition. In common with other masters of the past and present, Copland has undergone striking transformations in style over the course of more than thirty years. Throughout this period, largely because of his thorough, conservative, and rigid training, he has always been able to retain his individuality, and this has continued to be one of his strongest traits.

Only once did Copland waver, when he was caught in the wild eddies of Parisian ultra-modernism during the early twenties. Surrounded by composers who had swallowed its doctrines whole, and were turning out complex and detached combinations of dissonances in their terror of being considered emotional, and their desperate desire to be different at all costs, Copland conformed. Returning to his home town, he shocked musical New York with his artificial experiments—but not for very long. He soon realized that the new tenets to which he had subscribed were alienating the majority of the educated public, which was drawing back into a shell of cautious indifference.

"During these early years," he said, "I began to feel an increasing dissatisfaction with the relations of the music-loving public and the living composer. It seemed to me that we composers were in danger of working in a vacuum. It made no sense to ignore the vast new public created by radio, phonograph, and films, and to continue writing as if they did not exist. I felt that it was worth the effort to see if I couldn't say what I had to say in the simplest possible term."

Nurtured by his need to communicate, his eagerness to write music that would be identifiable as American, Copland's development was speedy and secure. His prolific production, from the utilitarian film scores to the chamber music and symphonies aimed at the most profound objectives, has established him as both the most distinguished and the most popular of American classical composers.

Two stages of Copland's career typify the bulk of the rest— the one that resulted in the noble and aspirational music based on ideas, such as "A Lincoln Portrait," and the one that motivated the unmistakably American ballet scores, "Billy the Kid," "Rodeo," and "Appalachian Spring," in which Copland displayed unique individuality in his picturesque and imaginative use of cowboy songs and hymn tunes.

Undoubtedly it is the indigenous and flavorful "rootin' tootin' and shootin'" scores that account for Copland's wide popularity, from which he has extracted his most effective and orchestrally inventive symphonic suites. Our recorded illustration is from "Appalachian Spring"—music as American as apple pie. ⬤ 148

There is hardly any phase of modernism, except that which disavows music's further ability to express human feeling, which Copland has not tackled. He has experimented recently with the twelve-tone techniques, and he also has had considerable experience utilizing jazz elements, which are found in his *Music for the Theatre, Piano Concerto,* and in a few other works. Finally, Copland declared that he was through with experimenting any further with symphonic jazz. "I felt," he said, "that I had done all I could with the idiom, considering its limited emotional scope."

Eventually, that is how Ravel, Stravinsky, and others who adventured with jazz, came to feel, but almost all of them were inspired to try their hand at it, under the influence of George Gershwin—the only composer of concert music who demonstrated decisively that jazz can be made the basis of estimable symphonic works.

While it would be naïve not to recognize Gershwin's obvious limitations and defects as a composer, it would be equally naïve not to recognize his unique achievements, which went far beyond the possibilities of technical craftsmanship. Gershwin had inspiration—the most indestructible element in art. Inspiration may appear in a march, a mass, or dance tune. It may prevail through a potboiler, or a masterpiece. It still provides the magic to which the great heart of the public responds. Gershwin's concert works possess that unanswerable power, and this is all he ever wanted.

When he came upon the scene in the early twenties, a high wall separated classical and popular music. Gershwin demolished it in 1924 with his *Rhapsody in Blue.* This was his key to immortality, and with it he unlocked the gate between concert music and the one form of art that is genuinely and indigenously American— the art of the Broadway musical.

Gershwin went on to fresh triumphs with his *Piano Concerto, An American in Paris,* and *Porgy and Bess,* his crowning achievement. The musical language he spoke was an eclectic one: in short, typically American. He had the conviction—and it may well symbolize his greatest contribution—that the finest service he could render his art, and the best he could do for himself, would be to write concert music that anyone could understand and enjoy for its own sake. Though we should not search for profundity or technical perfection when we listen to Gershwin's music, let us also resist adopting a patronizing attitude toward it. After all, it has demonstrated a vigor and stability usually reserved for only the proven classics.

An American in Paris is unquestionably a little gem—a chronicle fusing the fantasy and realism of a rhythmic melodist who made a trip to France and translated his experience into a giddy and inspired musical diary of nostalgic remembrances. Our illustration presents its spritely and nose-thumbing opening. 🎵149

The durability of *An American in Paris,* as well as of the *Rhapsody in Blue,* and the *Piano Concerto,* has been extremely puzzling to those who never quite certified Gershwin. The only possible explanation for this lies in the fact that Gershwin's music carries the expression of his environment with such force and accuracy as to explain itself to both the present and the future. Vital works always carry such evidence, no matter how much they may lack the completeness of a masterpiece. In Gershwin's case, it is all the more convincing because he was not the only one who essayed jazz in serious compositions.

To all other composers, jazz was a spicy ingredient mixed into fluffy souffles that were meant to be savored with tongue in cheek.

To Gershwin, it was a serious and sophisticated element of the eclectic language he spoke—a language that consisted of Lisztian pyrotechnics, Tchaikovskian sentimentality, blackface humor, Broadway pep, and French chic. It may surprise many to know that Gershwin was unequivocally hailed as "a great composer" by such uncompromising musicians as Ravel, Schönberg, and Stravinsky.

ELECTRONIC MUSIC

As we have observed, the musical art of the past three centuries is generally represented by two main types of composers: the evolutionists, with strong links to the past, and the revolutionists, who sought fulfillment through radical expansion or flat rejection of the established art. But whatever the degree to which artistic necessity drove composers to the alteration, extension, or repudiation of the deep-rooted language of music, not until recently did composers feel it necessary to discard its principles ruthlessly at each and every point, and to scrap completely the vocabulary in the work of their predecessors. In the musical art of the past two decades, we have witnessed not only the dethronement but also, in electronic music, the total renunciation of all former methods and means of producing, organizing, and projecting sound.

Although this new way of composing has inevitably produced various schools with diverse concepts and methods, some of them even diametrically opposed, their uniform purpose is the production of music based on the electronic transformation of sound. Whether instrumental, vocal sounds, or noises of indeterminate pitch make up the raw material, everything is recorded on tape and then subjected to a complete metamorphosis. It is speeded up, slowed down, played backwards, treated to an unlimited variety of distortions of pitch, timbre, duration, and dynamics. The results are then synthesized, spliced together, and finally coordinated into a desired structure. Editing techniques afford the composer—

or designer—a wider range of sounds and sound effects, much lower and much higher than any instrument could produce. Manipulation also provides endless opportunities for complexities of rhythm totally beyond the capabilities of any soloist or group, because the permutations are electronically, not humanly, produced. The chief performers in this new world of superhuman vibration are the playback machine and the loudspeaker.

Since the details of a technological development do not concern the music lover any more than other technicalities not experienced audibly, the proof lies in the sounds themselves. Perhaps their best-known creator, Pierre Boulez, the Parisian prophet of that branch of electronic music called "concrete music," proclaimed that Schönberg's twelve-tone system was as necessary to the future advance of music as it was inadequate to the solution of modern formal problems. His own solution was to expand Webern's rigorous and rarefied style by extending Webern's organization of the twelve-tone row to other musical components such as rhythm and structure.

The sounds of concrete music are so distorted, so reworked, that they are either difficult or impossible to identify. It is therefore a waste of effort and time to try to determine whether a baby's cry, a waterfall, or a cello is used to produce the original sound. But at all times, actual instruments or voices provide the raw material for concrete music.

The electronic world has, however, its own avant-garde, which insists that electronic music can no longer imitate sounds that are not electronically produced. A compendium of its goals and practices could be found in the work of the German, Karlheinz Stockhausen, who generates most of his material by purely electronic means and mixes his sound from three generators. In some early experiments, he combined the techniques of electronic music and concrete music by adding the traditional instruments and voices to his electronic base. Our recorded illustration shows some typical sonorities and patterns of Stockhausen. ⬤ 150

We now come to another branch of electronic music called "random music." As its title implies, each performer is allowed to improvise. The score is a diagram that supplies only specific time directions, but leaves just about everything else to each player, including the conductor, who thereby assumes the role of chronometer. We hear this disciplined anarchy illustrated in *Variations IV*, by the American John Cage, who has introduced new innovations made possible through the newest advances in electronic development, and who has exerted a tremendous influence upon a large number of young, avant-garde composers throughout the world. 151

What are we to make of all these curious sounds? Can we evaluate them as music when they shun recognizable harmonies and melodies and rhythms, and seem to have so little sense of momentum that they appear to have no determinable construction? If the answer is no, as I think it might well be to all but the "Annointed," why then is electronic music worth our consideration? For many reasons that cannot be lightly disregarded.

Whether we like it or not, whether it interests us or bores us, electronic music is with us and has been for a long time in some form or other. Its roots actually go back to the beginning of our century when a musical device was invented called the "dynamophone." Since then, many other apparatuses, very different from each other, have been developed with one objective in common— the mechanical creation of music in a scientifically perfect manner, free from all human and instrumental restrictions.

There is no denying that this objective has now been accomplished. The machine has revealed infinite possibilities beyond those of the human mechanism for manipulating sound. It has made it possible, for example, to divide with mathematical accuracy the twelve tones of the chromatic scale into quarter-tones, eighth-tones, or sixteenth-tones, and there is no logical reason why this should not be done. Today, the universe of sound is virtually unlimited in range, tone color, and dynamics, from the tiniest pianissimo to the most deafening fortissimo. This extension of the frontiers of sound is an inevitable upshot in our technological age, and sound being the raw material of music, it is not surprising that a large number of composers have attempted to employ the new technology to achieve artistic ends.

Although the various schools of electronic music are each cursed with their share of frauds who tend to debase the whole movement, we must be careful not to judge the movement by their efforts. The majority of composers working in the electronic media are honest and dedicated men of keen intellect, whose theories and disciplines have been developed with irrefutable logic. They believe sincerely that the great tonal art belongs to the past, and that whatever the human being can devise, the machine can do better.

The electronic movement is worldwide, and has earned the support of many respected individuals and institutions. Even the most radical schools of electronic music have been provided with technical and financial assistance from venerable universities and leading foundations. They have been given sound laboratories, subsidies for experimentation, inexhaustible supplies of magnetic tape, and two wondrous machines—the Synthesizer, which can synthetically produce any sound on earth, and a computer that can actually compose.

A large body of electronic music has resulted which has been subject to considerable exposure and evaluation. One segment of it has been widely and justifiably acclaimed for having successfully provided ideal accompaniments to the horror films and science-fiction productions of motion pictures and television. In short, electronic music has already demonstrated unique effectiveness as a background to appropriate dramatic situations.

In the concert hall, however, electronic music has aroused in most music lovers and critics a formidable amount of frustration and resistance. Attending a concert is a human as well as a musical experience. When we are moved and excited, it is not only the music but also its interpretation by a commanding personality which carries us out of ourselves and stirs something deep within us. No comparable experience is possible when an audience is confronted by a dehumanized loudspeaker that is either the sole performer or the dominant performer at a public gathering. This we know from dozens and dozens of events, even those presented under the glamorous auspices of major orchestras, even when the electrifying Leonard Bernstein has tried to dramatize the electronic credo.

But there is another reason, the crucial one, for the failure of electronic music as music. Its composers have produced no masterpieces. This is not surprising, for they are working in a new language that is still in an embryonic stage. But the public's business is still masterpieces—those affirmative, finished products that are as far beyond mere technical processes and theories as the plain man's subconscious response to them. The public's primary concern, as always, is with what has been done, not with how it has been done: with results, not with methods.

There are those who insist that the electronic composers are only summing up for our generation our own sense of emotional barrenness and spiritual despair; that in their machine-made and arid art, devoid of poetry and sensitivity, they are merely echoing the brutalizing forces in the world that seem to be destroying our permanent values. Others hold that these composers represent the wave of the future, and that all composers outside the electronic orbit are the disciples of decadence.

Neither view is convincing. None of us has the right to say that the experiments of our time, no matter how callow they may be at the moment, may not provide a genius with elements that may stir him to the creation of a convincing work of art. No one can tell what direction music will take: Geniuses have the disconcerting habit of transforming history in a way that no theorist can forecast.

What then is the music lover's responsibility? Quite simply, it is to avoid both indifference and faddism, and to participate vigorously in the age-old indispensable action of selection and rejection. The norms by which we gauge musical values, no matter what forms they take, remain substantially the same. It is not a crime to make a distinction between an unfledged attempt and a mature work of art: In fact, there is an urgent, healthy imperative to do so. Accidents called art, novelties, overworked dissonances, and electronic noises have all been with us for a long enough time. Hardly anyone is naïve enough to be frightened by them. Ironically, slavish adherence to inflexible and paralyzing conventions and repetitious manipulations have made the products of each fashionable system sound as much alike as if their makers were all busily engaged in writing warmed-over Tchaikovsky. The consequences were inevitable: The musical public may have become shockproof, but it has not become "boreproof."

Our age is likely to resemble all other ages in its handful of masterworks, its greater number of lesser but worthy works, and its overwhelming proportion of pure junk. It is highly probable that of all the music that is making such a big noise today, and I use the word advisedly, no larger or smaller share may survive than has survived the passing of previous eras. Assuredly, the first half of our bewildering century has brought forth a great many gifted composers, theorists of unquestioned importance, and at least its quota of geniuses.

The big men of the future will, as always, go their own ways, What directions they will take, what techniques they will use, cannot be predicted; but we can be sure that whatever elements they employ will remain merely elements, never substituted or mistaken for the whole. We can also be sure that a vibrant composition will soon be embraced by a tremendous public, grateful for one more artistic creation that speaks to the heart.

Come what may, I believe optimistically that we music lovers have considerable cause for good cheer—if only we will keep our minds and ears open for the vital works that make music a living language.

Index

Index

absolute music, 39, 70, 93
accents, 18
Afternoon of a Faun, The–
Debussy, 25
Agon–Stravinsky, 88
Aida–Verdi, 80
Albéniz, Isaac, 85
alphabet, musical, *see* musical
alphabet
American in Paris, An–Gershwin,
102
"American Quartet, The"–Dvořák,
78
"Annie Laurie," 36
"Appalachian Spring"–Copland,
100, 101
Appassionata Sonata–Beethoven,
50, 70
aria, 65
vocal, 41
atonality, 8, 89. *See also* tonality
"Awake My Love"–Dowland, 11

B-Minor Mass–Bach, 31
Bach, Carl Philipp Emmanuel, 42
Bach, Johann Christian, 42
Bach, Johann Sebastian, 7, 8, 9, 10,
40, 42, 71
absolute music of, 39
concerto principle of, 41
influence of, 39
solo concerto in, 63
use of fugue texture, 40
use of slow movement, 65
use of syncopation, 17
use of the scale, 14
use of vertical and horizontal

harmony, 31
ballet, 71, 75, 76, 87
Barber, Samuel, 99
Baroque style, 14, 31, 39, 65, 71
masters of, 42
Bârtók, Béla, 97
folk style of, 77
influence of, 92
rhythmic innovation of, 19
Beethoven, Ludwig van, 4, 18, 28,
29, 41, 43, 44, 50, 55, 60, 70,
71, 77, 93
development of melodic span,
38
influence on Bârtók, 92, *see*
Bârtók, Béla
orchestral influence of, 65
piano concerto openings, 66
rondo form of, 57
scherzo form in, 53, 54
sonata principle of, 43
symphonic methods of, 47
treatment of the finale, 58
treatment of the minuet, 52
use of key changes, 48
use of the coda, 49
use of the major scale, 10
use of the melodic minor scale,
11, 14
use of variation, 50
Benvenuto Cellini–Berlioz, 72
Berg, Alban, 90, 91
Berlioz, Hector, 24, 72
father of program music, 69
instrumentation of, 72
orchestral technique of, 71
scores of, 73

111